Leadership and Charisma

NEW HORIZONS IN LEADERSHIP STUDIES

Series Editor: Joanne B. Ciulla, *Academic Director, Institute for Ethical Leadership and Professor of Leadership Ethics, Department of Management and Global Business, Rutgers Business School, USA*

This important series is designed to make a significant contribution to the development of leadership studies. This field has expanded dramatically in recent years and the series provides an invaluable forum for the publication of high-quality works of scholarship and shows the diversity of leadership issues and practices around the world.

The main emphasis of the series is on the development and application of new and original ideas in leadership studies. It pays particular attention to leadership in business, economics and public policy and incorporates the wide range of disciplines which are now part of the field. Global in its approach, it includes some of the best theoretical and empirical work with contributions to fundamental principles, rigorous evaluations of existing concepts and competing theories, historical surveys and future visions.

Titles in the series include:

Paradox and Power in Caring Leadership
Critical and Philosophical Reflections
Edited by Leah Tomkins

Rethinking Leadership
A New Look at Old Questions, Second Edition
Donna Ladkin

William Shakespeare and 21st-Century Culture, Politics, and Leadership
Bard Bites
Edited by Kristin M. S. Bezio and Anthony Presti Russell

Judgment and Leadership
A Multidisciplinary Approach to Concepts, Practice, and Development
Edited by Anna B. Kayes and D. Christopher Kayes

Leadership and Charisma
A Cultural-Evolutionary Perspective
Micha Popper and Omri Castelnovo

Leadership and Charisma

A Cultural-Evolutionary Perspective

Micha Popper

Professor, Department of Psychology, University of Haifa, Israel

Omri Castelnovo

Lecturer, Department of Psychology, University of Haifa, Israel

NEW HORIZONS IN LEADERSHIP STUDIES

Edward Elgar
PUBLISHING

Cheltenham, UK • Northampton, MA, USA

Published by
Edward Elgar Publishing Limited
The Lypiatts
15 Lansdown Road
Cheltenham
Glos GL50 2JA
UK

Edward Elgar Publishing, Inc.
William Pratt House
9 Dewey Court
Northampton
Massachusetts 01060
USA

Paperback edition 2023

A catalogue record for this book
is available from the British Library

Library of Congress Control Number: 2021952734

This book is available electronically in the **Elgar**online
Business subject collection
http://dx.doi.org/10.4337/9781802203523

ISBN 978 1 80220 351 6 (cased)
ISBN 978 1 80220 352 3 (eBook)
ISBN 978 1 0353 2039 4 (paperback)

Printed and bound by CPI Group (UK) Ltd, Croydon, CR0 4YY

For Rinat

Contents

Acknowledgments

Writing a book is usually a long process that involves many factors. It always starts out with a specific idea or insight, but only in rare cases does the idea remain in its original form. Particularly, complex phenomena that have no single definite explanation – and leadership, followership, and charisma are certainly known as phenomena of this kind – tend to arouse curiosity, and generate extensive discussion, frequently provoking many arguments and disagreements.

Indeed, this book represents a developmental process, years in the making. Apart from the personal journey, the book's claims were crystallized through much in-depth reading, by countless conversations between us and those students who conducted their research under our guidance and supervision and, of course, through contact with the numerous people who talked to us or read early drafts of the manuscript, and whose comments enlightened us in many ways. The final version of the book is the result of small and large inputs, of random corridor conversations and lengthy discussions. It is difficult to enumerate all the people who have contributed. Some are not even aware of their contribution (for example, an insight born out of a random conversation which occurred in an elevator, in the space of time it takes to descend four floors ...).

Therefore, our heartfelt thanks go out to many. We cannot even pretend to mention them all. We would like to thank the following people who we simply asked to dedicate their time – either in conversation or in reading drafts.

Professor Dan Jacobson from Tel Aviv University, a colleague and friend, for his encouraging enthusiasm after reading a very early draft of the book.

Dr. Rami Dovrat, a friend of many years – for his referrals in the fields of psychology and anthropology.

Professor Baruch Nevo from the Department of Psychology at the University of Haifa – a friend and colleague, for his insightful comments following a thorough reading.

Professor Danny Koren, a friend from the Department of Psychology at the University of Haifa, who was involved in leading research and writing articles based on the ideas presented in the book.

To our students who participated in a series of studies that were based on the ideas discussed in the book: Yahal Geffen, Michal Frostig, Niv Quart, and Chen Harush.

Dr. Brigadier General Meir Finkel, for his insatiable curiosity and knowledge in both biology and evolution, which provided us with important insights in the context of leadership.

Dr. Dan Asher, student and colleague; Professor Tzur Shapira, a colleague from New York University; Professor Ofra Nevo, our friend from the Department of Psychology at the University of Haifa, who read early drafts or parts of them and encouraged our efforts.

To all of our friends involved in the field of leadership or who have great interest in it, who provided us with insightful feedback and valuable advice: Eliav Zakay – CEO of "Lead"; Gadi Amir, Boaz Amitai, Moshe Siegel, Ronen Gavish, Shai Satran, and Dan and Ada Sever.

To Sharon Erez, our English editor, for her work and, most of all, her constant willingness "to be there" whenever help is needed.

To our family members who always know how to help – both in words and deeds: Rinat Popper and Naomi Kedar, and Oria Castelnovo. We thank you all from the bottom of our hearts!

1. Introduction to *Leadership and Charisma*

POINT OF DEPARTURE

In the TV series, *The Crown*, about the British royal family, a dialogue is presented between the young Queen Elizabeth, who is facing her coronation as Queen, and her husband, the Duke of Edinburgh. The Queen, on the advice of the royal court veterans, wants to perform the ceremony as it has always been conducted – as a "sacred" ceremony that takes place away from the public eye in exactly the same way, with the same rituals that have always existed like other religious rituals.

Her husband suggests changing the ceremony, in the spirit of "the changing times". He suggests broadcasting it on television to make it more popular, more transparent, and less attached to the historic protocol. The main difference between the two approaches focuses on the following arguments:

The Duke of Edinburgh: People want to see their heroes as flesh and blood people – "up close", with all their weaknesses.

The Queen: People want to see us being exalted, above the people. They do not want to perceive us as ordinary people because this detracts from the "comforting effect" that royalty has on people.

This dialogue reflects various assumptions about the attitude of followers toward leaders. Do followers have a tendency to romanticize leaders – to see them as a desired story?[1]

The book deals with this riddle. It examines the roots at the base of *leadership as a phenomenon*. Particularly, it focuses on people's strong attraction to leaders, as a result of their "charismatic nature". Such an examination begins with the fact that leadership is not an exclusive human phenomenon; leadership also exists among many animals. Animals whose lives are conducted in flocks also have a social hierarchy; yet, as is discussed in the book, despite common foundations, human beings have unique manifestations regarding the phenomenon of leadership.

Charisma is, first and foremost, associated with strong emotions. It is sometimes likened to falling in love,[2] and as with falling in love, it has a subjective element. It can exist in the eyes of followers at some point and disappear later. If charisma is claimed to be a phenomenon "in the eye of the beholder", the obvious question is: Why hasn't research focused more on followers – specifically, on the sources and purposes of their longing for and attraction to leaders? That is, on the patterns of the followers' construction of leadership images?

Such an observation requires a theoretical, out-of-the-box approach – an effort that is always extremely difficult. As is well known, the most natural tendency is to follow an established path – certainly this is the case in research that typically relies on previous studies, similar to relying on precedents in the legal world.

The point of departure for the presented discussion is that leaders are only part of the leadership phenomenon, which needs to be examined along with two additional components: followers and context. A metaphor that has greatly influenced us is the one that likens leadership to fire. Fire is ignited by the leader, who is the spark. However, it ignites various combustible substances that differ in the degree of their combustion potential. Some followers are more "flammable" than others. The combustion itself – the duration and height of its flames – is fed by oxygen, which feeds the fire – in this case, the environment and the circumstances.

So, what is the cause and what is the outcome of this fire/combustion process? Is it an interaction? If so, what is its nature? These are complex questions which the book discusses. Moreover, there is a genuine need to clarify issues given the claim that most comparative research on human behavior is mainly focused on countries referred to as WEIRD societies (Western, Educated, Rich and Democratic), which represent 80 percent of the research and only 12 percent of the world population.[3] The meaning of this disproportion is, of course, clear with regard to the generalization of findings. But beyond that, it is possible that in general, the reference to certain phenomena is cultural, and therefore any comparative bar is problematic in the first place. A book that dealt with cultural influences on the perception of visual stimuli showed that people from different cultures perceived visual stimuli, or parts of them, in a way that derived from their culture.[4] If this is the case with visual images (which are supposed to be objective and universal stimuli), it goes without saying that there is a problem with studies of more complex phenomena.

Here is another illustration of the meanings of partial or biased sampling in the context of medical care. A recent television article presented a case in which symptoms such as pressure in the chest area, left arm pain, and difficulty breathing – "typical signs" of a heart attack, which usually cause people to rush to the emergency room – are not necessarily relevant signs of a heart attack in women.

The TV article presented evidence of women who thought they had heartburn, came to the emergency room and received heartburn medication, but had actually experienced a heart attack.

How does such a diagnostic error occur? The explanation provided by medical experts is that the vast majority of subjects in medical research in the field of cardiology are men. Thus, the ever-improving treatment methods following technological advancements (such as MRI, for example), and the development of sophisticated statistical software, which can achieve incredible levels of accuracy and measurement, may be biased and even erroneous, only because the point of origin is the over-representation of men. If this is the case with regard to specific visual stimuli or diagnostic medical data, obviously, it is even more complex when it comes to psycho-social phenomena. Charisma is just one such phenomenon, and probably one of the most elusive.[5]

Indeed, a bird's eye view of the history of leadership research[6] raises the well-known association of the Indian parable of the elephant and the group of blind men, in which each blind man touches and recognizes a single part of the elephant's body – trunk, foot, and so on – each "sees" something different, and none succeeds in identifying the animal as an elephant. The danger of reduction – of seeing trees while ignoring or failing to even look at the whole forest – can lead to conceptual biases and inaccuracies.

Moreover, many who watch movies about Hitler or Jim Jones – the leader of a cult that convinced 911 of its members to commit suicide – wonder how these men could have had such a tremendous amount of charisma. To many, they even look ridiculous. Such perplexity accompanies us in many observations of leaders. Even in daily conversations about politicians, there is often a debate about the charisma of leaders: whereas some perceive a particular leader as charismatic, others simply cannot see the attraction.

These examples and questions make it clear, at the most simplistic intuitive level (at this point), that charisma is first and foremost a great influence on people. Singers, actors, or lecturers can also be charismatic in the sense described.

The book focuses on charismatic leadership – a phenomenon which, in our opinion, is not only psychological and anthropological, but has evolutionary foundations and a role in the intergenerational development of groups. Moreover, in recognizing charismatic leaders in human history, such as Nelson Mandela or Benito Mussolini, it cannot be said that charisma is necessarily a "good thing". It can promote non-violence (Mahatma Gandhi), but it can just as easily promote destruction and devastation (Adolf Hitler). And as with infatuation, charisma is not necessarily stable; it can exist for a period of time and later disappear.[7] If charisma is, as we claim, a phenomenon which is "in the eye of the beholder", then why does the research literature not deal more with the observers – the followers – the patterns of their emotions and unconscious echoing to figures perceived as charismatic?

This book attempts to answer this question and others: Why are we attracted to leaders? What are the universal and cultural components which underlie our "falling in love" with certain leaders? Why are we attracted to different types of leaders? Why do we perceive certain leaders as charismatic? Why are some leaders more charismatic in our eyes than others? Why do those leaders who are perceived as charismatic in one period, stop being perceived as such in another period? Or vice versa: those who are not perceived as charismatic leaders become more charismatic during other periods. Why do some leaders become "forever charismatic" beyond time and place, while others who were extremely charismatic in their time fall into the abyss of oblivion and are all but forgotten?

The book's uniqueness lies in the fact that it perceives leadership as an inherent ingredient rooted in the "evolutionary software" of humankind. This does not mean that the leadership of a lioness leading a band is like the leadership of a state leader, team leader, or corporation leader. There are common elements; however, it is clear that there are also differences explained by the unique development of human beings.

In this sense, this book is not "another book on leadership", but rather an observation of a phenomenon that is essentially too complex to be understood through a single disciplinary lens. The book presents a perspective that integrates evolutionary, psychological, sociological, and anthropological angles, all of which shed light (also through historical observation) on a phenomenon that exists in every society, large and small.

The beginning of the journey is in evolutionary observation. From there, it is possible to follow developments that clarify the components underlying human leadership. The analysis clarifies what, in the phenomenon of leadership, can be generalized beyond all cultures and which elements in this phenomenon are culturally bound.

THE CONCEPTUAL FRAMEWORK

Leadership is one of the most discussed and researched phenomena. A review of the literature on leadership research indicates the clear dominance of American literature on leadership.[8] This literature often presents leaders as cultural heroes: remarkable independent individuals, entrepreneurs, revolutionary pioneers, courageous figures, and so on. These are not random descriptions. They typify American culture, which has glorified individualism from an early age.[9]

In one study, social psychologists Hazel Markus and Elissa Wurf[10] describe the same situation – that of a mother feeding her small child – in the United States and Japan. To her son who refuses to eat, the American mother says things like, "Don't you want to be a famous basketball player?"; and "How will you be strong enough if you don't eat all your food?" In the same situation, the Japanese mother tells her small son about the many people who prepared the food: the cowherd who milked the cow, the person who turned the milk into cheese, the people who packed the cheese, the driver who drove the cheese to stores ... Finally, she asks: "Do you not respect the efforts of all these people who were busy preparing food for you?" And so, from early childhood, different norms, such as individualism and collectivism, are internalized. Such norms are also later expressed in reference to leaders.

Literature about American organizations depicts the leadership of managers like Jack Welch (CEO of General Electric) as icons presented in the business press and US business schools as role models. On the other hand, successful Japanese companies, like Toyota, emphasize the "method" rather than the leaders.[11] Hence, cultural differences, as the Dutch organizational researcher Geert Hofstede showed,[12] can paint the images of leaders in different colors. This, of course, casts doubt on the ability to generalize arguments about leadership.

As noted, such insights have led us to search for patterns whose understanding can contribute to the distinction between the universal and the local-cultural aspects in the discussion of leadership. To do this, we start from the beginning – the evolutionary observation that makes it possible to examine what can be generalized beyond the different cultures, and what requires understanding of cultural and situational contexts. Important insights for this analysis include those described in the subsections below.

Discussion of Leadership Is Essentially a Discussion of the Phenomenon of Followership

The literature has dealt extensively with leaders. Hundreds of biographies have been written about leaders such as Washington, Lincoln, Mahatma Gandhi, Ben-Gurion, and Ata Turk, among others – generators of national revivals or dramatic upheavals, who have become both national mythologies and symbols of collective identity. Such stories are so popular that it has become a genre of written history. For example, James McGregor Burns – whose monumental book, *Leadership*,[13] is considered one of the most influential books in the field of leadership studies – was actually referred to as a "presidential scholar", as he specialized in writing biographies of US presidents (especially the Roosevelts). The fact that biography is perceived as an inferior genre of historical research, but the most popular when it comes to sales,[14] indicates that people are biased in favor of personal stories.

American psychologist, Jerome Bruner, noticed this love of stories in humans.[15] This tendency is visible and direct among children, but in fact no less so among the "older children" – the adults. The fact is that most of us eagerly read stories about people and their lives in novels, gossip magazines, and weekly supplements; and watch TV shows that are personal and intimate with great interest. The story of Albert Einstein's life, for example, interests most people more than his claims about cosmology.

Within this propensity for life stories, leaders' stories are probably more fascinating than those of most other known people while stories about leaders who were "scoundrels" are probably even more fascinating (similar perhaps to the attraction to crime drama heroes?). The books written about Hitler, for instance, are more numerous than those written about most of the leaders in human history.

The esteemed British historian, Ian Kershaw, who wrote, according to many, the most comprehensive biography of Hitler,[16] wrote in the introduction to the book about the different approaches to historical research and his dilemma in writing – which ranged from the structural approach to focusing on the man himself. Kershaw claimed that the concept "charismatic leadership", as discussed by Max Weber, helped him to integrate the different approaches. "If I have found one concept more than any other which has helped me find a way to bind together the otherwise contradictory approaches through biography and the writing of social history, it is Max Weber's notion of 'charismatic leadership'."[17] Charisma, as deployed by Weber, is "a notion which looks to explanations of this extraordinary form of political domination primarily in the perceivers of 'charisma', that is, in the society rather than, in the first instance, in the personality of the object of their adulation".[18] That is, those who seek explanations for the extraordinary influence of charismatic leaders, argues Kershaw, should seek it in society and not necessarily in the personality who is the object of admiration.

There is another aspect that Kershaw raised in his descriptive reports, but did not sufficiently relate to its full psychological implications: The influence of followers on the self-expectations and self-image of the leader. At the beginning of his political career, Hitler saw himself, as he wrote in *Mein Kampf*, as a "drummer" – calling the masses to the banner of the "national movement". At that time, he still did not see himself as the future leader of Germany, but rather as one who paves the way for the great leader whose time might come in many years. As he told his associates, "I am nothing more than a drummer and rallier (Trommler and Sammler)."[19]

He explains he was not the leader and statesman who would "save the Fatherland that was sinking into chaos", but only "the agitator who understood how to rally (sammeln) the masses". He added that he was not "the architect who clearly pictured in his own eyes the plan and design of the new building and with calm sureness and creativity was able to lay one stone on the other. He needed the greater one behind him, on whose command he could lean."[20]

All that, however, changed over time. The mob's admiration for him as a speaker at the Munich mass rallies changed his self-image and self-expectations. He began to believe he was, indeed, that great leader – the one who would save and glorify Germany. As the social psychologist and leadership researcher, Boas Shamir, noted, there is evidence here of a process that requires a change in focus – from the leader figure and his needs toward understanding the needs of the followers.[21]

Leadership literature has mainly dealt with one direction of influence – the leader's influence on his/her followers. This, however, is a partial and perhaps even distorted perspective. Leaders are greatly influenced by the dynamics and expectations of their followers. In some cases, this is even the key to understanding their impact.

Followers Have Inherent Biases in Processing Information Concerning Leaders

The most common bias followers have in their attitude toward leaders is the tendency to give more weight to people than to processes – a bias known as "fundamental attribution error" in the field of social psychology.[22] For example, in a well-known study,[23] people were asked to choose one out of four different reasons to explain the success of events. All reasons were equally probable. However, most people chose leadership as the explanation for the success. People, for example, almost exclusively attributed the upheaval that took place in the Soviet Union to Gorbachev. Much less weight was given to economic or social processes (e.g., the long decline of the Soviet economy, which showed that the "system" did not work).

Such biases are also conspicuously evident in election campaigns in the Western world. Most people do not analyze social, economic, or geopolitical processes when it comes to voting in elections. The majority does not even read the parties' platforms. The real choice, in fact, is about the leader who heads the party – a clear manifestation of the fundamental attribution error. This bias intensifies the more distant the leader figure is. The less the leader is subjected to direct observation, the greater the subjective elements in constructing the leader's image. This is part of the general patterns found in social psychology studies that deal with "psychological distance".[24] For example, a study conducted among American students presented them with a possible occurrence that could happen in the near/distant future: "In a few days/years, the university will be prepared to increase the quota of minorities admitted to the university." Students were then given a list of statements (e.g., preparation of potential candidate lists) expressing an ideological-moral reference (e.g., reducing inequality in society, justice). It was found that ideological-moral references were more common in the context of the distant future. The closer the situation was in time, the less the ideological/moral references were mentioned.[25]

The principle according to which construal of objects, events, and people is more abstract the more distant they are is particularly conspicuous when it comes to images of leaders. Boas Shamir[26] demonstrated some important aspects of this argument. In his study, 320 students from The Hebrew University of Jerusalem were interviewed. They were asked to describe a leader who had no direct contact with them – a "distant leader" (81 percent of the distant leaders were political leaders), and to describe a leader with whom the interviewee had direct contact and acquaintance – a "close leader" (28 percent of them were teachers, 26 percent were commanders whom they knew personally from the army, and 24 percent were friends). Comparing different characteristics between the images attributed to distant and close leaders, it was found that there was a greater wealth of characterizations regarding close leaders, and these characteristics were more specific and more behavioral (e.g., expressions of expertise, personal example) compared to those attributed to distant leaders, which were described in more abstract and simplified terms (e.g., social courage and ideological orientations). The distant leaders were sometimes described as "larger than life". Indeed, some scholars have argued that distant leaders are more prone "to processes of romanticization and mythologization".[27] Abraham Lincoln – the most revered president in the history of United States – became an icon of charisma only decades after his death. He is a clear manifestation of a mythological story. Had there not been some leading newspaper editors in the early twentieth century, Lincoln would probably have sunk into the abysses of oblivion.[28] Dead Lincoln is undoubtedly more charismatic than living Lincoln.

In terms of the psychology of followers, this description points to two phenomena that have been extensively discussed in psychology: (1) *projection* and (2) *attribution.* Although the two terms differ, they both point to the same direction of human ability in the context of leadership: the ability to construct characteristics of "greatness" (power, wisdom, etc.) and relate them to certain entities and figures. This ability, which is probably unique to humans, generates a sense of confidence and calmness, and even reduces oppressive emotions such as guilt feelings.[29] From this point of view, God for example, is the ultimate leader. To millions of believers, he can be exactly what his followers want him to be. The figures who are considered close to him (Muhammad, Jesus, Moses) are known as the most charismatic leaders in human history.[30]

Thus, projection and attribution are central psychological mechanisms that allow people to "anoint" leaders. This ability is related to primary and universal needs – such as security, which seems prominent in situations of crisis, uncertainty, and change; and symbolic needs – related to meaning, and to personal and group identity.

Appointing Moshe Dayan, the most famous Israeli General in the 1960s, as Minister of Defense on the eve of the Six Day War, under public pressure (contrary to the preference of then-Prime Minister Levy Eshkol), is an example of two previously discussed processes: (1) the search for a "great figure" that provides a "response" to collective existential anxieties (Dayan enjoyed the aura of a successful chief of staff); and (2) symbolic and culturally bound processes: the almost unconditional trust given to leaders from military backgrounds in Israeli society (part of the ethos of a nation that fights for its existence).

Indeed, leaders have a symbolic power, which explains followers' attraction to different figures in various cultural groups. In an experiment we have been conducting for many years among students and in training workshops on leadership, we begin with an "opening exercise": we ask participants to name leaders. It turns out that most of the chosen leaders are mentioned by all of the groups. For example, Churchill, Mahatma Gandhi, John F. Kennedy, Abraham Lincoln, Ata Turk, Hitler, Nelson Mandela, Ben Gurion, and Yitzhak Rabin always appear on every list. Therefore, it can be said that these names are a representative sample – the personification of leadership as a phenomenon.

After writing the names on the board, we try to find the "organizing principles" at the basis of the phenomenon that has been reflected by the class. What quickly becomes clear is that it is difficult to find common patterns and behavioral rules. Some leaders are characterized by their outstanding rhetorical ability (e.g., Hitler), while others are stutterers (e.g., Yitzhak Rabin). Some are good looking (e.g., Kennedy), while others are not considered to be particularly attractive (e.g., Gandhi). In short, no single visible characteristic can be pointed out as a "threshold condition" or prerequisite for becoming a leader. However, this discussion changes when analyzed from the perspective of the followers' needs. Then, the basic contours of the phenomenon become clear: the need for security and direction, and the centrality of the feeling that "there is someone to trust". These emotions commonly come to the fore, and will be dealt with more extensively in the following chapters.

Interestingly, when presenting this request to Orthodox Jews who grew up within what can be described metaphorically as a "cultural island", detached from the dominant culture, a different pattern emerged. The leaders indicated are rabbis (e.g., Rabbi Kook, Rabbi Solovitchik, Rabbi Ovadia Yosef) and other religious, folkloristic figures such as the Baal Shem Tov and the Rabbi of Lubavitz).

These examples illustrate three principles that will be expanded further. (a) The phenomenon of leadership is also culturally bound and associated with the symbolic world of the group. (b) Learning about leadership is greatly influenced by the figures we are exposed to in our socialization processes. (c) Belief in the leader as a symbol empowers the group. These principles have many implications for "leadership consumption" processes, which are part of a broader phenomenon of the intergenerational transfer of symbols. Anyone who has visited a Chabad (a distinct group of Orthodox religious Jews) synagogue can see these principles in action – in the constant storytelling and wonder surrounding the figure of the Lubavitcher Rebbe. This is basically a process of romanticization and mythification of the leader. Such processes can be found in many cultures and are part of an understanding of the phenomenon of leadership in general, and charismatic leaders in particular.

It seems that one basic process becomes clear: the more distant the leader is from the followers, the more s/he is the manifestation of the followers' projections and attributions. The leader is presumably a story, sometimes mythological, that serves the followers' different needs. Such aspects of "constructing leaders" have been partially studied in the leadership literature. They were mainly presented in writings in which leadership was analyzed using psychodynamic theories relating essentially to unconscious processes, or in studies grounded in social-psychological theories dealing with various social information processes. The result is hundreds of studies that do not provide a wide enough view into the phenomenon of leadership as a whole.

After much deliberation, we thought that in order to reduce "researchers' biases", "school-of-thought biases", or "cultural biases" it might be insightful to return to the fundamentals that exist in nature. That is, to rely on the same reasoning underlying many developmental studies which assumes, for example, that toddlers have not yet been influenced by social or political socialization. In short, we focused on defining the initial and authentic elements in the phenomenon of leadership. However, we argue that understanding these foundations is not the "whole story", but it helps to understand the origins of differential attitudes toward leaders which are ostensibly only "cultural".

The Phenomenon of Leadership Is Primarily Emotional

Another insight that comes from turning the spotlight on the followers is the centrality of emotions in the discussion of leadership. Ignoring or reducing the reference to the emotional component in early studies in social sciences in general, and in the research on leadership in particular, is probably due to the centrality and prestige of researchers and research in the natural sciences. It is well known that the founding researchers in psychology aspired to adopt the way of thinking and research methods that characterizes the natural sciences. For example, researchers such as Fredrick Skinner and Kurt Lewin were clearly considered more "scientific" as they conducted lab experiments and dealt with measurable variables.[31]

The streams in psychology that clearly dealt with emotions, such as the psychoanalytic school of thought, were controversial in the academic world. Proponents of Freud and his successors also saw the psychodynamic arguments as "thoughts" and the practices derived from them as "art", rather than science. Indeed, for many years, paradoxically, psychology – the discipline that is assumed to deal with human nature – has reduced research interest in aspects that are not only typical of human beings – in some cases, they are unique to them. "Compassion", "love", "hate", "friendship", "jealousy", "revenge" – the very core issues of which life is composed – were not at the forefront of research. People pondered and discussed these aspects through novels, films, and plays.

True, there have been developments in this regard in recent years, but this may be due to the maturation of technologies that advance neuropsychological research capabilities. Evidence is growing on correlates of empathy in the brain; studies are being conducted on the effect of oxytocin on social emotions, and so on. This is a trend that has hope and perhaps promise for understanding worlds that were not at the forefront of research. Still, the findings are essentially correlational, while the big integrative picture remains largely enigmatic.

One way or another, there is undoubtedly a greater degree of legitimacy today for engaging in a field called "emotions research". A number of today's universities have research institutes that focus on the study of emotions. Interdisciplinary collaborations in the study of emotions exist, and even issues like interstate or intergroup conflicts are being explored from theoretical perspectives that deal with emotion regulation.[32]

Associating emotion with evolutionary sources was discussed impressively in a theoretical paper published about 40 years ago by Stanford University's social psychologist, Robert Zajonc.[33] This paper argued that, in many cases, emotion "jumps" prior to processing information in the brain.

One of the most helpful and common distinctions in recent years is the distinction between system 1 – a decision-making system that is fast, emotional, and "uncalculated" (falling in love); and system 2 –which is responsible for calculated decisions (buying a car or investing in the stock market).[34] We argue that emotions are central in choosing leaders and following them. This is especially conspicuous during election campaigns. We will dedicate an analysis to this specific situation.

To sum up the general claim in broad terms, it can be said that looking at leadership and followership from the perspective of "backward inquiry" ultimately leads to the foundations that characterized the beginning of human evolution. Some of these factors are universal and common to all humankind (e.g., fear of snakes[35]), while others are group-level factors that have evolved into intercultural differences.[36] In the book, these links are discussed at length, within the context of leadership and followership.

The general argument is that the initial attraction to leaders is universal. Those individuals experienced by others as most able to address the group's fundamental, existential needs are perceived as more attractive. Those who transmit particularly prominent signals in this context will be experienced by others as more charismatic – that is, they will have a particularly strong impact. From where do such signals derive their appeal? What is behind the influence of people we experience as charismatic? What is at the core of the electrifying impact of, say, Martin Luther King's "I Have a Dream" speech? What caused Rev. Jim Jones's followers to commit suicide and even kill their children? We should note that such phenomena are not uncommon in our history, as is clearly seen in literature, films, plays, and other art forms. And yet, it is very difficult to explain this impact.[37]

Throughout the book, we will try to show that the gap between the prevalence of the experience of a strong influence, and the ability to explain it in research, is not accidental. We will present the possibility that it is difficult to explain such an effect, without exceeding the level of analysis we usually use to explain the conventional rules existing between human beings in daily life. This may be the reason for the Greek origin of the word *charisma* (God's gift) and our "magical" attributions toward it. It is no coincidence that this phenomenon is considered "irrational", surprising, and contradictory to our beliefs about free will. This happens because it is a phenomenon that belongs to different rules, which are beyond observed daily conduct. These rules are associated with aspects that serve humans, but humans do not define them. It is based on the foundations of the human *race* as a whole, rather than on interpersonal differences. This argument may contribute to a more modest and careful approach to everything that is described in the leadership literature in terms of "unusual greatness".

The difficulty in a discussion on prominent universal signals associated with evolutionary claims stems from the fact that charismatic leaders do not have objective and identical contours that are always generalizable beyond different collectives (such as height). Charisma is also related to symbolic differences between groups, such as differences between national cultures. Evolutionary observation can also shed light on the source of these differences and how they came about.

As is well known, the human individual was neither the strongest nor the fastest creature in the struggle for survival. His adaptive advantages stemmed largely from his ability to work in a group. *Homo sapiens* developed a culture (language, norms, practices) that made the choice of leaders and the attachment to them more complex, compared to the initial attraction to leaders based on the primary adaptive needs. However, looking at the cultural development of different groups points to an evolutionary logic illuminating the formation of different images of charisma. Although Gandhi is an Indian leader, the underlying explanation for his development into a symbol – a charismatic leader – has a rationale that is related to characteristics of Hindu culture. This argument is relevant to leaders in other cultures as well. The symbols of different collectives (including images of leadership) are distinct and unique to different collectives. However, the *need for symbols is universal*. Its foundations are anchored in the evolution of the group. The book describes these processes and how they are related to leadership and followership.

THE BOOK'S STRUCTURE

Chapter 2, "Evolution and sensitivity to signals", presents the theoretical point of departure, anchored in an evolutionary paradigm. When the word "evolution" is mentioned, the immediate associations that arise are the thoughts and theories of Charles Darwin. However, beyond his observations about biological evolution, Darwin's way of thinking has contributed greatly to theoretical developments in various fields – from the social sciences to disciplines such as computer science.

Darwin's ingenious observations focused the world's attention on living organisms' ongoing adaptation processes in relation to the environment. This view requires the ability to relate to different layers that were not addressed at the same level of conceptual and empirical analysis. For example, the research that developed following Darwin's ideas emphasized *biological* adaptation in different environments, including weather, geographical, and geological aspects. However, Darwin's ideas were not fully utilized in this context.

In his reference to the environment in *On the Origin of Species*, Darwin introduced the idea of "spaces in the natural economy", now known as "niches", that are different in terms of abundance and availability of resources that create different adaptation conditions. The well-known concept of "variation" is therefore also relevant at the level of intergroup differences and has been attributed with multiple ways of explaining intercultural differences between human groups that developed in various adaptive niches.[38] Such observations can, of course, shed light on the different preferences and sensitivities of different groups (such as why some societies are more collectivistic, while others are more individualistic).[39]

Furthermore, in many cases, the transfer of adaptive knowledge is not detailed enough beyond biological expression. For example, in an experiment in which cat hair was left among mice that had never seen a cat, they responded with a panic-and-escape response. This was not their reaction when dog hair was left near them. Thus, it would seem clear that some knowledge is passed down from generation to generation.[40]

Evolutionary observation can expand our understanding of intergenerational learning, which is more complex than the initial evolutionary ideas. Emotions, norms, and cultural knowledge can also be transferred through intergenerational processes. Such ideas can be traced, for example, in Jung's ideas on cultural archetypes or in Max Weber's theory on religious values passed down from generation to generation – values that affect attitudes toward work and lifestyles.[41] This idea is also echoed in works on emotions passed down from generation to generation as a result of collective trauma, such as among survivors of the European or Armenian Holocaust.[42] These examples suggest that "biological" hardware is not the entire story. Apparently, emotional and cultural aspects also have an impact on intergenerational learning.[43] This point is central in trying to explain social phenomena such as leadership.

The literature that has developed around these issues is enlightening in that it shows cultural evolution among various collectives; however, it is lacking at the micro level. That is, it does not focus on the following questions: How does this learning occur? How do cultural norms and practices actually pass from generation to generation? Attempts to explore and conceptualize these intergenerational learning processes have evolved greatly over the past two decades[44] and have significantly contributed to the development of the arguments presented in the book regarding the ways in which charismatic leaders influence followers.[45]

Leaders are described by many scholars in terms of identity, loyalty, and group patriotism. There is a general romanticization of leaders in every collective. However, going back to the beginning of the development of *Homo sapiens*, prior to the formation of language, indicates that leadership began as the simplest coordination mechanism of group activity,[46] which is basically the foundation of any organization. As the organizational researcher, Henry Mintzberg, pointed out in his work, organizations can be classified according to their coordination mechanisms. In small organizations, the manager-leader can clearly be seen as fulfilling a key coordinating function.[47]

Concepts in contemporary literature about leadership such as "direction", "alignment", and "commitment"[48] are expressions concerning a means by which to improve this primary and universal function. In other words, the development of the language and the symbolic abilities of *Homo sapiens* enabled the existence of more abstract, more complex channels of communication. However, at their core, they serve an ancient purpose – group coordination.

This claim will be further elaborated in the discussion regarding the universal foundations of leadership as a catalyst for two adaptive axes: (1) a horizontal axis of coordination and synchronization that contributes to group cooperation through coping with present adaptive challenges; and (2) a vertical axis comprised of knowledge and the group's symbols transferred over generations.

These universal aspects are sometimes blurred because cultural differences are reflected in different images of charismatic leaders.[49] For example, the American researchers, Gerstner and Day, compared leadership perceptions among student population in eight countries. They presented the subjects with 59 leadership characteristics and found that the degree of agreement about them was so small that they could not indicate leadership "core images" around which there was clear agreement. Moreover, none of the top five leadership characteristics found in the US sample was ranked as the top five in the other samples.[50]

In an interview, an Israeli researcher, who grew up in Turkey and specializes in Turkish culture, characterized the cultural aspect of the Turks' attitude toward their highly controversial (in the West) leader, Erdogan. In answer to the interviewer's question: "How do the Turks come to terms with the thousand-room palace Erdogan built, with his private plane, and his masses of servants?", the reply was: "Turks are not Israelis. Think of the Ottoman Empire – the Turks are used to sultans living in palaces. Ataturk also lived in a palace in Istanbul. For the average Turk, it is natural for a ruler to live in a palace; it is not considered a sign of corruption. On the contrary, it shows that the country is glorious, that it has power."[51]

However, these differences regarding the sensitivity of different collectives to different symbols should not obscure the common principle that groups need shared, unifying symbols – both for their cohesion and resilience in the present (the horizontal axis) and as a basis for preserving this resilience in the future (the vertical axis). As will be elaborated, leaders serve this universal need by being both agents and "manufacturers" of unifying symbols.

This discussion also illustrates a central idea discussed in the book at length: the idea of *signals*. The book's focus is not on leaders' personality characteristics, but on which signals experienced by followers are perceived as relevant enough to "anoint" some individuals (more than others) for leadership positions. There are several prominent signals that particularly help followers identify leaders. Some of the signals, as mentioned, are universal and are clearly and closely related to basic existential needs, while others are acquired during cultural learning processes. Understanding the dynamics of these signals illuminates the combination of the universal and cultural elements underlying the influence we call "charisma". This is a central argument in the book, exemplified through various studies and examples, some of which are well known in human history.

Chapter 3, "The attraction to leaders", focuses and expands the discussion on the signals that are experienced by the followers as "signs of leadership". The chapter presents two types of signals: the first signal concerns the primary needs in adaptive processes. These signals are common among all animals who perceive a certain individual animal as being more capable than others of helping them face environmental threats. At the more primitive levels, such signals reflect physical strength. At the more complex levels, these signals are more sophisticated, but they point to the same need – a response to threats and challenges.

Through the presentation of studies and historical examples, the chapter describes the leadership signals that are most prominent in two situations: in times of crisis and during election campaigns. Our instinctive sensitivity to such signals (despite all attempts at denial) illustrates that we are, indeed, "part of the world of animals". The analysis also indicates other processes with evolutionary "logic" that clarify when the "magic" of these signals expires, or rather which conditions allow the magic of these signals to continue to exist over long periods of time.

The second type of leadership signals are not seemingly directly related to individual biological instincts, but are acquired developmentally over time. That is, these are signals that can evoke emotions in one group, and not necessarily in another. This is similar to symbols in different areas of life such as a flag, football team, or songs which evoke different emotions in different groups. Leadership is also a symbolic trigger that evokes differential emotional responses.

Prior to the discussion on the impact of such signals, an attempt is made in this chapter to pinpoint the concept of "culture" in the specific context of the discussion on followership. Culture is analyzed here in terms of the typical reactions expressed in regard to preferences and decision-making – aspects that are almost automatic and, as stated, common to a particular group, but not necessarily to another group (e.g., different ethnic groups). This chapter focuses on the aspects relevant to characterizing the cultural signals of leadership.

Chapter 4, "Charisma", "mobilizes" the insights presented in previous chapters regarding "leadership signals" in order to demonstrate and analyze significant cases of charismatic leadership. We use a basic schema we call "neediness and greatness" – a generic schema that describes, for example, the relationship between a baby (a "needy figure") who sends out "distress signals" when he is scared or hungry; and a caregiver (a "large figure") who responds to these distress signals. Different interpretations of this schematic state have been proposed in hundreds of studies conducted in the field of developmental psychology, particularly in attachment studies.[52] A review of leadership studies also indicates the existence of this type of schema in reference to leaders. Such an initial schema is especially evident in crisis situations. In such cases, the effect of primary universal signals is clearly seen in followers–leader dynamics.

However, this is not the whole picture. Humans acquire and carry with them down the road sensitivity to cultural cues. This sensitivity is essential to the "consumption" of leadership and charisma. This argument is exemplified by some known historical cases that serve as a "magnifying glass" that clearly shows the variables and processes discussed. Among the studies and examples discussed in the chapter, the discussion on Hitler was somewhat expanded. This is because: (a) this is an example of a prominent charismatic leader; (b) the circumstances of its occurrence provide an abundance of empirical data which is hard to find for other charismatic leaders; and (c) despite the above, the interpretation of Hitler's charisma is complex and multidisciplinary, and presents conflicting arguments. Using the complex example of Hitler enables the presentation of a more comprehensive look at the principles underlying the phenomenon of charisma.

Chapter 5 discusses key issues that the book's arguments did not cover or which may imply assumptions that need to be considered. Observing followership as one of the cornerstones for understanding the phenomenon of leadership, and analyzing the psychological and evolutionary processes underlying followers' need for leaders naturally raise the following questions: If the evolutionary default is to be a follower, then who are the leaders? And why do some individuals emerge from this "automatic pattern" as leaders, while others do not? This is the first issue discussed in the chapter.

The second issue expands the discussion in a context that is much more complex than the paradigm common to "regular" adaptive processes among animals. Human beings have an exceptional ability to learn. This aspect makes the discussion much more complex compared to other mammals' adaptation issues. Consequently, leadership among humans is more complex to analyze compared to any other animal, let's say, leading the herd. Understanding human followership and leadership is related to the combined effect of phylogenetic components (those more universal components that are related to the development of the species as a whole) and symbolic components (acquired and culturally unique). Clarifying this general claim (which may be somewhat obscure at this point) through examples and research is actually at the book's core.

Finally, we provide a recommendation regarding how to read and relate to the contents of the book. We will first present the rationale for this recommendation: some phenomena are simply more "Gestaltic" than others. That is, the whole picture is larger than the sum of its individual parts. For example, seeing a beautiful woman does not necessarily imply that every part of her face is perfect. Sometimes, looking at each part individually detracts from seeing the beauty in its entirety. In our eyes, leadership and certainly charisma are also examples of such phenomena. Up until now, research in this area has always focused on specific variables and in many cases, as noted, on variables that are easier to observe and measure (those variables that are "in the spotlight"). Metaphorically speaking, reading this book may be likened to reading spy novels or detective stories. Each chapter adds information, but the big picture – the "putting together" of all the cumulative pieces of information – only becomes completely clear at the book's end. At least we hope so.

NOTES

1. Bruner, Jerome (1986). *Actual Minds, Possible Worlds*. Cambridge, MA: Harvard University Press.
2. Lindholm, Charles (1988). Lovers and leaders. *Social Science Information*, March, 27(1) (March), 3–45.
3. Henrich, Joseph, Heine, Steven, and Norenzayan, Ara (2010). The weirdest people in the world? *Behavioral and Brain Sciences*, 33, 61–135.
4. Segal, Marshal H., Campbell, Donald T., and Herskovits, Melville J. (1966). *The Influence of Culture on Visual Perception*. Indiana, IN: Bobbs-Merrill.
5. Popper, Micha (2001). *Hypnotic Leadership*. Westport, CT. Praeger.
6. Bass, Bernard M. (2008). *The Bass Handbook of Leadership*, 4th edn. New York: Free Press.
7. Popper, Micha (2012). *Fact and Fantasy about Leadership*. Cheltenham, UK and Northampton, MA, USA: Edward Elgar.
8. Bass, *The Bass Handbook of Leadership*.
9. Popper, *Fact and Fantasy about Leadership*.
10. Markus, Hazel and Wurf, Elissa (1987), The dynamic self-concept: A social-psychological perspective. *Annual Review of Psychology*, 38, 299–337.
11. Liker, Jeffrey and Hoseus, Michael (2008). *Toyota Culture: The Heart and Soul of the Toyota Way*. New York: McGraw-Hill.
12. Hofstede, Geert (1997). *Cultures and Organizations. The Software of the Mind*. New York: McGraw-Hill.
13. Burns, James MacGregor (1978), *Leadership*. New York: Harper & Row.
14. Shapira, Anita (1997). *Yehudim Hadshim, Yehudim Yeshanim*. Tel Aviv: Ofakim, Am Oved (Hebrew).
15. Bruner, *Actual Minds, Possible Worlds*.
16. Kershaw, Ian (1998). *Hitler, 1889–1936: Hubris*. London: Penguin Books.
17. Ibid., p. xiii.
18. Ibid., p. xiii.
19. Ibid., p. 169.
20. Ibid., p. 170.
21. Shamir, Boas (2007), From passive recipients to active co-producers: Followers' role in the leadership process. In B. Shamir, R. Pillai, M.C. Bligh, and M. Uhl-Bien (eds), *Follower-Centered Perspectives on Leadership*. Greenwich, CT: Information Publishing, pp. ix–xxxix.
22. Ross, Lee D., Amebile, Teresa M., and Steinmatz, Julia L. (1977). Social roles, social controls and biases in social perception processes. *Journal of Personality and Social Psychology*, 35, 485–94.
23. Meindl, James R., Ehrlich, Sanford B., and Dukerich, Janet M. (1985). The romance of leadership. *Administrative Science Quarterly*, 30, 78–102.
24. Liberman, Nira, Trope, Yaakov, and Stephan, Elena (2007). Psychological distance. In A.W. Kruglanski and E.T. Higgins (eds), *Social Psychology: Handbook of Basic Principles*. New York: Guilford Press, pp. 353–84.
25. Ibid.

26. Shamir, Boas (1995). Social distance and charisma. Theoretical notes and explanatory study. *Leadership Quarterly*, 1, 19–48.
27. Meindl, James, R. (1995). 'The romance of leadership as follower-centric theory: A social constructivist approach', *Leadership Quarterly*, 6, 329–41.
28. Schwartz, Barry (2000). *Abraham Lincoln. Forge of National Memory.* Chicago, IL: University of Chicago Press.
29. Kets de Vries, Manfred (1988). Prisoners of leadership. *Human Relations*, 41(31), 261–80.
30. Popper, *Fact and Fantasy about Leadership.*
31. Skinner, Fredrick (1965). *Science and Human Behavior.* New York: Free Press. Lewin, Kurt (1947). Frontiers in group dynamics: Concept, method, and reality in social science. *Human Relations*, 1, 5–42.
32. Halperin, Eran (2014). Emotion, emotion regulation, and conflict resolution. *Emotion Review*, 6(1), 68–76.
33. Zajonc, Robert B. (1980). Feelings and thinking, preferences need no inferences. *American Psychologist*, 35(2), 15–175.
34. Kahneman, Daniel (2017). *Thinking Fast and Slow.* New York: Farrar, Straus & Giroux.
35. LoBue, Vanessa and DeLoach, Judy S. (2008). Detecting snake in the grass: Attention to fear-relevant stimuli by adults and young children. *Psychological Science*, 19(3), 284–9.
36. Boyd, Robert and Richerson, Peter (1988). *Culture and Evolutionary Process.* Chicago, IL: University of Chicago Press.
37. Antonakis, John, Bastardoz, Nicolas, Jacquart, Philippe, and Shamir, Boas (2016). Charisma: An ill-defined and ill-measured gift. *Annual Review of Organizational Psychology and Organizational Behavior*, 3, 293–319.
38. Howard, Jonathan (1982). *Darwin.* Oxford: Oxford University Press.
39. Tallhelm, T., Zhang, X., Oishi, S., Shimin, C., Duan, D., Lan, X., and Kitayama, S. (2014). Large-scale psychological differences within China explained by rice versus wheat agriculture. *Science*, 344(6184), 603–8.
40. Panksepp, Jaak (1998). *Affective Neuroscience: The Foundations of Human and Animal Emotions.* Oxford: Oxford University Press.
41. Weber, Max (1924/1947). *The Theory of Social and Economic Organization*, reprinted 1947, trans. Talcott Parsons. New York: Free Press.
42. Vamik, Volkan (2016). *Siblings.* Charlottesville, VA: Pitchstone Publishing.
43. Boyd and Richerson, *Culture and Evolutionary Process.*
44. Csibra, Gergely and Gergely, Gyorgy (2009). Natural pedagogy. *Trends in Cognitive Sciences*, 13, 148–53.
45. Castelnovo, Omri, Popper, Micha, and Koren, Danny (2017). The innate code of charisma. *Leadership Quarterly*, 28, 543–54. Popper, Micha and Castelnovo, Omri (2018). The function of great leaders in human culture: A cultural- evolutionary perspective. *Leadership*, 14, 6, 757–74.
46. Van Vugt, Mark, Hogan, Robert, and Kaiser, Robert B. (2008). Leadership, followership, and evolution. *American Psychologist*, 63(3), 182–96. Van Vugt. M. and Grabo, Allen E. (2015). The many faces of leadership: An evolutionary-psychology approach. *Current Directions in Psychological Science*, 24(6), 484–9.

47. Mintzberg, Henry (1973). *The Nature of Managerial Work.* New York: Harper & Row.
48. Drath, Wilfred H., McCauley, Cintya D., Palus, J. et al. (2008). Direction, alignment, commitment: Toward a more integrative ontology of leadership. *Leadership Quarterly,* 19, 635–53.
49. Hofstede, *Cultures and Organizations.*
50. Gerstner, Charlotte and Day, David (1994). Cross cultural comparisons of leadership prototypes. *Leadership Quarterly,* 5, 121–34.
51. An interview with Dr. Hai Eithan Inrojack, *Haaretz* Supplement, November, 30, 2018 (Hebrew).
52. Bowlby, John (1973). *Attachment and Loss, Vol. 2: Separation.* New York: Basic Books.

2. Evolution and sensitivity to signals

ON SIGNALS THAT EVOKE PRIMARY EMOTIONS

On December 11, 2016, a tragedy occurred that shook the Israeli public. During a family trip in the Negev desert, hikers, including Dr. Omri Nir and his son Eli, descended a ladder down into one of the wadis. The son, Eli, slipped off the ladder. His father, in the blink of an eye, jumped off the ladder in an attempt to catch his son and keep him from falling. They both fell into the creek far below. Dr. Nir managed to shield his son and absorb most of the blows while falling, but died as a result. His ten-year-old son died two days later in the hospital.

In retrospect, it is clear that if the father had done some "situation assessment" (or any other term used in theory and research on decision-making processes), he probably would have concluded that his impulsive leap could not have saved his son. This case, however, turns out to be not as unusual as one might think. There is ample evidence of parents running into burning buildings to try and save their children trapped in the fire – even when it is abundantly clear to everyone witnessing the incident that this is a futile act[1] – which when analyzed retrospectively is clearly "irrational". In such situations, there is no way to calculate the cost–benefit considerations so typical in economic or strategic writings.[2]

Reservations about the dominance attributed to "rational thinking" have been presented in various writings, but it seems that they have intensified in recent years, particularly in the areas of research focusing on judgment and decision-making processes.

Probably the best-known reservists in the modern age are the scholars Daniel Kahneman and Amos Tversky (who received the Nobel Prize for their joint work).[3] Kahneman candidly said that he wanted to present their initial ideas to a famous professor in order to get feedback on the direction he and Tversky were developing. After hearing the basic ideas, the professor muttered that he did not want to evaluate works on "the stupidity of human beings". However, as the two claimed, they were not at all dealing with the stupidity of human beings.[4] They were, rather, engaged in what they called: "biases in information processing". Here is an example of the type of experiments they conducted:

Respondents were asked the following: Person A is waiting in line at the movie theater. When he arrives at the box office, he is told that he is the millionth customer and has won $100.

Person B is waiting in line at another movie theater. The person in front of him arrives at the ticket office and is told that he is the millionth customer, and has won $1,000. Person B gets $150 for being next in line right after the millionth customer.

Would you rather be Person A or B?

The expectation of any person who thinks "economically" will probably be that a reasonable (wise, rational, etc.) person will prefer to be Person B – who gets $50 more than Person A. In practice, however, most people say they prefer to be Person A, and actually make an irrational decision to give up an extra $50 – just to avoid the bad feeling that can result from knowing they were so close to winning a thousand dollars.

This example illustrates, among other things, that Kahneman and Tversky's contributions dealt with well-defined issues that were empirically researched. However, neither the creative questions underlying their research nor the strictness of their experiments brought them world fame. What did bring them worldwide recognition was the decisive illustration that people, as in the example above, systematically "do not act logically".

When people lose $50, they do not feel the same as when they gain $50. Although it is the same amount in both situations, their response is not identical. People tend to be much more irritated by loss situations. Losses affect the human psychology much more than gains on a similar scale. When most people react in this way, as Kahneman and Tversky and their successors have shown, it is not a matter of collective stupidity, but rather a *systematic* bias of information processing. What the researchers found in their experiments is something more powerful and influential than the clearly expected gain. This is called *loss aversion*. When people consider dilemmas of the type presented, they tend to focus on losses rather than profits. Such a consistent pattern obviously has implications for the world of financial investment, stock market behaviors, and so forth. Indeed, in a long series of experiments Kahneman and Tversky found several biases that provide insights into how people think and process information. Thus, two psychologists became the founders of the field called "behavioral economics" (Kahneman received the Nobel Prize in Economics).

Identifying such biases, when they are patterned – that is, appear among most people – significantly affects the way people think, decide, and behave. Using medical imagery, such biases can be perceived as symptoms. If most people are characterized by the same symptoms, it is worth thinking about the reasons why this is so. Why do human beings constantly make decisions that are seemingly contrary to their visible self-interests?

If we examine, for example, the bias of "loss aversion" from an evolutionary perspective, it will be quite easy to come to the conclusion that such a bias is derived from origins that are deeper than "here and now" dynamics.

In a series of experiments conducted at Yale University,[5] researchers gave Capuchin monkeys tokens, which they could use to "buy" delicious apple slices. The monkeys quickly learned to use tokens like money. But then the researchers added a twist to the study: different people offering different offers. The first person always showed the monkey one slice of apple and gave it to him for one token. The second person always showed the monkey two apple slices, but gave him only one in exchange for a token. From an "economic" point of view, both people offered exactly one apple slice in exchange for a token. But the second person, by offering two slices but giving only one, focused the monkeys on what they lost – the second apple slice. The monkeys significantly preferred the first person, although from an economic point of view, as mentioned, the second person offered exactly the same deal. Just like humans, monkeys hate the feeling of loss. Since the same pattern appears in monkeys and human beings, it can be assumed that there is an evolutionary basis for this reaction. In evolutionary terms, many of the seemingly irrational decisions humans make are not stupid at all. Most animals live very close to the edge of survival. Scholars of ancient cultures have discovered evidence that our ancestors coped for long periods with scarcity, subject to the folly of nature.

What guided their behavior was attempts to minimize the threat of not having enough food to survive. In other words, sometimes there is a rationale for human behavior that not only cannot be *explained* by "contemporary logic", but may actually run counter to it. Biologists refer to this as *ultimate factors* – factors that existed in the early stages of human evolution. A clear example of this is humans' great attraction to high-sugar foods, which are not only high-calorie and fattening, but – as we now know – also harmful to our health.

However, at the beginning of the evolutionary process, high-calorie foods helped our ancestors to store energy and survive in an environment where nutritious foods were rare.[6] Although humans' living conditions have changed and are no longer similar to those of our ancestors, the development of the human brain is not in sync with these types of developments. Changes resulting from evolutionary developments are known to be very slow. Indeed, a variety of findings by anthropologists, biologists, and culture researchers suggest that the decision-making process in humans today is still sometimes aimed at advancing ingrained evolutionary goals. This is a different type of logic whose basis for understanding is ancient.[7]

This logic is hard to accept. However, hundreds of studies show that the roots of human and social behaviors that we tend to explain by cause and effect explanations in the short term have different logic when analyzed with an evolutionary perspective.

According to this argument, the biases revealed by Kahneman and Tversky are not errors that indicate defective thinking. These are rather responses resulting from the evolutionary development of the brain designed to test real evolutionary challenges. When it comes to danger and disease, our brain is geared toward hypersensitivity to strangers, and any sign of disease or danger.

In short, there are two general principles in the evolutionary process which are common to all animals: (1) somatic effort; and (2) reproductive effort. *Somatic effort* (soma = body health) is the energy that an animal expends to grow and maintain a healthy body. *Reproductive effort* is the energy invested in gene replication. The somatic effort is like making a deposit in a cumulative account in an individual's bank – building health. The reproductive effort makes it possible to create offspring – a deposit in the bank account of the species. Examining these two efforts illustrates the differences between various animals' strategies. Some creatures (usually the smaller ones) tend to have a strategy to reproduce faster, while others (usually the bigger ones) tend to have a strategy to reproduce slower. For example, the Tenrec (a hedgehog-like mammal found in Madagascar) lives on a fast track, and reaches sexual maturity four days after birth. Tenrecs give birth to huge numbers of offspring (up to 32 at a time). Elephants, on the other hand, are slow to sexually mature, and even after they are physically ready, they may wait additional years before producing offspring.[8]

Humans, of course, are also on the slow path. They invest heavily in somatic development and wait many years for sexual maturation. And even then, most people will wait another few years until they decide to have children, in whom they invest a great deal of resources. Although babies have big brains, they are helpless for a long period of time. They develop slowly and are not able to live and develop without the help of caregivers. The helplessness of the human baby, of course, necessitates dependence on "great figures", without whom the baby could not have existed. Thus, dependence on these figures is experienced (and probably even embedded) from the very beginning. These types of primal feelings, as will be analyzed, are relevant in our reference to other authority figures encountered at later stages in life – leaders.

This inquiry back to the earlier sources of human existence sharpens the observation of contemporary emotional dynamics, including the observation of the leader–follower relationship, which has an ancient basis in the development of human beings.

To present this argument clearly, we will turn to the emotional areas that most people experience in one way or another: love, marriage, and raising children. For example, it has been found that men prefer to marry spouses who are younger than they are, while women prefer men who are older than they are. This preference is not a cultural matter as was previously assumed; it exists in traditional societies as well as in Western societies. For example, researchers who looked at personal ads around the world, found that men of all ages everywhere preferred women in their early twenties. Even 15-year-old boys fantasized about college-age women, age 18–22. The explanation that men give for this attraction is related to *signals*, such as smooth skin, and so on (powerful motives in the cosmetics and fitness industry ...). The early twenties is the most fertile period for women – not only do women get pregnant more easily at this age, this young age also implies many future child-bearing years to come. Even if a man does not explicitly want children, the argument is that his brain is wired to these signals.[9] Such an observation can also explain other phenomena associated with courtship relationships – ostentatious behaviors such as buying luxury cars – signals that radiate an economic capability, which may be perceived as a "factor of attraction". This type of signal also existed in ancient times, when the most muscular and strongest hunters were more attractive to women.[10]

The above examples illustrate the basic fact that we are surrounded by signals that contain information. Responses to signals that are more in line with the evolutionary principles presented will be faster and more homogeneous, compared to responses to signals that are further away from the biological-evolutionary source. Responses to the latter will usually be related to acquired and learned signals (which we will expand on below), and they will reflect more interpersonal and intercultural differences.

Thus, for example, the male peacock's glorious tail is nothing but a "signal", inviting female peacocks to mate and reproduce. This is a clear example, because the peacock's magnificent tail comes with a "price" in relation to survival – it is burdensome and thus reduces mobility and agility. But this price has a purpose. It makes it difficult or daunting for "scammers" to imitate the male peacock and win the female's attentions. Thus, the heavy price is an indication that the signal is both authentic and reliable.[11] A woman's young body contains signals (difficult to counterfeit) that evoke more homogeneous brain responses in men because they are "more evolutionary".

One of the distinctions that helps identify a signal as evolutionarily valuable was made in the famous article by Stanford University researcher Zajonc,[12] who claimed that signals related to emotions (to the limbic system) provoke response more quickly than other informative signals (related to the upper part of the brain – the cortex, which also developed later). This hierarchy has an evolutionary explanation. For example, the emotion called "fear" was crucial to survival. Anyone who did not "feel fear" – fast enough and accurately enough – was doomed to extinction.

An experiment conducted by LoBue and DeLoach[13] showed that people identify snakes faster than they identify other stimuli (the rapid detection of a serious threat leads to enhanced survival). People identified a snake among flowers more quickly than other stimuli placed among the flowers. To test whether this is indeed an evolutionary inherent tendency, the researchers gave the same task to 120 children, aged 3–5, who had never seen a snake before. In the first experiment, a snake among the flowers was presented in comparison to a flower placed among snakes. Both adults and children recognized the snake more quickly.

In the second experiment, a snake was placed among frogs, that is, among other animals. Also in this experiment, the snake was detected faster than the frogs. In the third experiment, the snake was placed among larvae, which were similar in shape to the snakes. In this experiment as well, the snake was detected more quickly than the larvae. Such experiments well illustrate the nature of an "evolutionary signal". This is characterized by the following facts: (a) it is not possible to indicate where and how the reaction was learned; and (b) the response to the signal cannot be explained in terms of visible cost–benefit considerations.

Indeed, as Zajonc noted, the emotional element (which is, as mentioned, more deeply related to "evolutionary signals") is central to human responses in many areas. Let's take, for example, the theme of "love" – which is perhaps the most emotional of all in the modern age – an unfailing source of endless songs, books, plays, and movies.

From an evolutionary point of view, love reflects a distinctly sexual element, as do all mating animals. Some animals mate without any emotion, exhibiting no signs of affection, no "personal attitude", not even an acquaintance with or responsibility toward the offspring. The sexual act is designed only to bring forth offspring (such as in the example of the Tenrec mentioned above). This element is biological. On top of this tier, there is an emotional element among some mammals. This is the basis for "falling in love" – the feeling that we have met someone who is different. This includes the feeling that we have met "someone suitable", who is perceived as more attractive than others.

The soaring divorce rates, the abundant evidence of many people who seem to experience an unhappy married life, alongside a multiplicity of expressions of infidelity (in the sexual sense) all indicate that the signals conveyed and perceived in the infatuation phase are not always enough to maintain a strong marriage over many years. The researcher, Ada Lampert,[14] clarifies the various layers of the phenomenon of love in humans through an evolutionary analysis. The sexual lowest tier is common to all. While feelings of falling in love are more typical among humans (especially in the modern age, where "romance" has taken precedence in the mating process), these feelings do not have an equal "evolutionary status" between men and women.

Simply in terms of supply and demand, a woman's egg is infinitely rarer and more precious than a man's sperm. Moreover, as with many of the females in nature, the female is often the one who is more emotionally associated with the offspring, caring for them, and raising them. Thus, there is a distinct asymmetry (of biological origin) between men and women. The investment of women in every sense is immeasurably greater than that of men.

If so, why would a man want to commit to one woman instead of "having fun" with many women? The reason for this also stems from an evolutionary rationale, according to which among the human race descendants have great significance as the carriers of genetic continuity. However, herein lies the trap. The male, because of the ease with which he can fertilize many females, is in a situation where he has no certainty as to the question of which offspring are his. And so, according to these explanations, the woman's desire for her offspring's security, and the man's desire to be sure that he has produced and is caring for his own offspring, are at the foundation of various arrangements of attachment between men and women.

When young people in the infatuation stage are asked why they are in love, they give answers like: "We are sexually attracted to one another"; "We enjoy doing things together", and so on. When adults who have lived together for many years and have children are asked why they are in love, the typical answers are: "He (She) is my friend. He/She is a great parent"; "He/She is a responsible person who can be trusted", and so on – answers that are not necessarily identical to the feelings that existed during the initial "falling in love" stage.

Indeed, in earlier periods in history, matches were arranged by the parents, according to elements that included economic and social considerations. The centrality of romantic, "Hollywood-style" love, is a relatively new phenomenon and it certainly poses the question (that will be discussed in the context of leaders and followers) of how reliable certain signals actually are. Or rather: *How can we examine the accuracy and reliability of signals?* An evolutionary analysis can help with understanding such an issue.

The method of observation demonstrated thus far can provide an organizing theoretical framework for the findings of Kahneman and Tversky's research with which we began the chapter. Just the title of Kahneman's book, *Thinking Fast and Slow*,[15] reflects an important distinction between two modes of response: The fast "System 1" response, and the slow "System 2" response.

In popular lectures (on television, for example) in which there is no time for detailed explanations, Kahneman demonstrates the difference between these systems by asking the audience to respond to the question: "How much is 2 times 2?" The audience immediately responds: 4. "And how much is 17 times 12 and a half?" Kahneman continues. After not receiving an immediate answer, he says: "To answer this, a calculation must be made and it will take time." On a descriptive level, this is the simplest difference between System 1 and System 2.

System 1 thinking is immediate and fast, while System 2 thinking is much slower and is characterized by data processing, inferences, and conclusions. When we buy an apartment or a car, most of us make calculations and assessments that characterize System 2 thinking. On the other hand, when we talk about "love at first sight", our way of thinking and the inferences that characterize our expression come from within and are immediate – all of which reflect System 1 thinking. In other words, some responses simply occur quickly, instinctively – without us dwelling on them, without considering them. Other responses depend more on examining and weighing the available data and alternatives. The source of the differences between these response patterns lies in the rationale presented – the weight of the evolutionary component instinctively experienced in the signal revealed to the observer.

The father who jumped to his death, although there was no chance of rescuing his son who had fallen from the ladder; the desperate parent's attempt to rescue his child trapped inside a burning house; the immediate sense of "ignition" we feel for someone in a romantic encounter are all examples of reactions that characterize System 1 thinking. The further away from the evolutionary component in the observed signal, the less rapid the reaction usually will be. For example, a person walking for pleasure along the river will jump into the river at record speed if his small child walking next to him falls into the river. His reaction will be less rapid, when a distant acquaintance falls into the river and even hesitant, if a stranger, whom he does not know, falls into the river.[16]

The closer we are to someone, the more they are "our flesh and blood", the faster our reactions will be – as if we have some kind of internal formula that almost chemically determines the speed (and type) of our responses to signals that contain information of differential evolutionary value.

This "jumping into the river" example illuminates another aspect of the evolutionary perspective: that of the *group* and its ability to support the survival of individuals. In his observations, Darwin identified the patterns of natural selection in nature. As is well known, the sentence that made him a glamorous icon among the general public was drafted following an article written by Thomas Malthus, a priest and scholar, who watched as Europe's terrible plagues claimed the lives of tens of thousands of people. In an essay (which became famous as a result of its use by Darwin), Malthus argued that there is an asymmetry between the demographic increase in the number of people, and the increase in food that can feed them. The number of people grows much faster than the amount of food required to feed them. This creates a situation where there is increasing and intensifying competition for ever-decreasing amounts of food. In this situation, "the strong (or fittest) survive". This is what many refer to as the "Darwinist principle".

It is this principle of constant competition for subsistence resources that is probably behind the tendency for mutual coordination and groupness in different species, especially humans. This evolutionary tendency, for coordination and cooperation purposes among individuals, confers clear survival benefits. It lies in the genetics of the human race and is already present at birth, but its influence branches out and is perfected later in life through learning and socialization processes. The result, as we shall see below, is a biologically learned complex that has fascinating implications for the leadership phenomenon as well.

Indeed, developments in evolutionary thinking have expanded the discussion and the range of Darwinist principles to a group level – first still in the realms of biological boundaries, genetic proximity, and later, in the human context – to issues more removed from individual biology (e.g., cultural evolution). One way to discuss the meanings of the expansion of evolutionary thinking is through signals that evoke different types of reactivity. As mentioned, the more "biology"-oriented information they contain, the faster and more homogeneous the response to them will be. The more distant they are from the "biological", the less homogeneous they are likely to be.

This can perhaps be clarified through the classic distinction (presented in every basic Introduction to Psychology book) that points to a hierarchy between primary needs and higher needs. Primary needs are related to hunger, thirst, sex, and security. Most animals in the wild come into the world with impressive abilities to recognize signals that help them satisfy these needs. However, other needs are associated with more complex dimensions, some of which are learned in the process of socialization, and some of which are combinations between the innate and the acquired.

The theoretical link between the different concepts presented can be clearly seen. The rapid responses (usually within the framework termed "System 1") are related to the sensitivity inherent in us regarding aspects relevant to primary needs such as the fear of snakes, the attraction to the power that gives confidence, and so on. The examples and studies discussed thus far testify to the "activation program" that was imprinted in us during the evolutionary process. As we shall see, part of the attraction to leaders stems from this ancient "software".

However, this direct connection to a leader is not the whole story. As human beings, we also have additional sensitivities that are activated in the encounter with social and cultural signals. We will now discuss the characteristics of these signals.

ACQUIRED SIGNALS

We will follow the sequence of the historical development of evolutionary thinking. As mentioned, an important branch that developed from Darwin's ideas focused on groups characterized by genetic proximity. Naturalists sought explanations for phenomena that clearly indicated there was greater complexity to the first evolutionary principles. For example, there was room to explain phenomena such as the existence of butterflies of the *Danaus plexipuss* type that are preyed upon by birds. Nature has favored these butterflies with both wings – which allow evasion – and with a bird-repellent scent – a scent recognized by the bird only after the first bite. This may seem to pose a problem; however, the *Danaus* also has a body that can withstand the bird's first bite; so ostensibly, the existential problem is solved. However, this is not the case with larvae (which have not yet matured into butterflies). The larva is a "delicacy" for the bird; its body is soft and it cannot fly. Furthermore, larvae tend to congregate with members of the same species; thus, a group of larvae could easily become an easy feast for the birds.

Why then, in practice, doesn't this happen? The answer is "family". Family members are genetically related. A hungry bird sticking its beak into a mass of larvae will hit one larva. It will leave the others to their own devices because of the disgusting smell following the bite. The first, unfortunate larva, sacrifices its life for the sake of its brothers and sisters. Natural selection, as researchers have argued at this stage of evolutionary thinking, produces a means of defense to ensure that more of the genes they share will continue to live in the bodies of those siblings whose lives have been saved.[17]

From here, it was an easy leap toward observations that emphasized the benefits which the group provides to the individual. For example, Emerson[18] placed ten sets of termites on absorbent paper, alongside ten separate creatures, and showed that the sets lost less water than the individual creatures. This proves that collaborative aggregation helps to cope better with arid environments where water is essential. A similar pattern is found among starfish.

As noted, the initial thinking about evolution and genetics did not touch upon the matter of grouping. However, research and evolving theory had to explain why blood-sucking bats share fresh blood at the end of the night with their flock-mates, who had an unsuccessful hunt; why vigilant deer jump high when they see a lion, thus drawing the attention of the predatory animal to themselves;[19] and why whales do not abandon a whale injured by whale hunters, even if by doing so they endanger their own lives.[20]

It is possible that both animal communities and human communities are ultimately part of the same developmental process itself. Individuals respond to their environment by grouping together, which gives them a survival advantage. In addition, the group members slowly learn to get along with the others developing trust, coordination and finally cooperation.

This direction gives significant weight to (1) grouping and the ability to cooperate, as well as (2) the ability to learn – two aspects that undoubtedly provided benefits to humans. Recent studies have indicated that not only do humans likely have an innate tendency to congregate in a group, they are also very sensitive when it comes to distinguishing between "my group" and the "other group". For example, brain studies have shown that cells in the brain produce increased electrical activity in encounters with strangers.[21] This ability exists even before adults "brainwash" their children with distinctions related to differences in dress, color, or manners. Indeed, it was found that 14-month-old infants tended to mimic more infants in their own group compared to infants from another group.[22] Experiments conducted among three-year-old toddlers before significant social or cultural socialization found that these toddlers have the ability to identify social categories.[23]

Evolutionarily, this inherent ability is of special value as it enables two advantages: (1) the reduction of threats, that is, distinguishing quickly who is "on our side" and who might be dangerous; and (2) the rapid identification of creatures that can be relied upon for the purpose of preserving and sustaining the resources required for existence and livelihood. The "grouping instinct" and the unique learning ability of humans are major reasons for *Homo sapiens'* victory over animals which were much more powerful and agile. The evolution of language 70,000 years ago, which by no means surpassed other animals, dramatically advanced humans' communication abilities – which developed into powerful abilities whose impact was far beyond the "here and now" dynamics.[24] Unlike the tiger, the lion – and in fact most animals that identify threats and opportunities concretely only within[25] their range of sight or hearing – human beings are better at conveying the "news" that "a lion was seen by the river" (when it is at a considerable distance) than most animals. That is, humans have the ability to detect and report threats from a great distance. Moreover, human beings do not necessarily have to see their "meal" hiding behind a tree to activate the attack-and-capture mechanism. In ancient times, humans already had the ability to study and understand their victims' behavioral patterns, which allowed them to devise a good plan and develop a clever and appropriate ambush.

"Learning", "delaying of gratification", "planning", and "cooperation" mechanisms characterize the human race more than other species, and form the initial infrastructure for building what we call "culture". An instructive example of this was presented in a study published in the prestigious journal *Science*.[26] In the study, members of a cultural group characterized by a high level of individualistic values were compared to another group, characterized by a high level of collectivistic values.[27]

An analysis of the sources of the intercultural differences of the two groups in the study indicated that the founding fathers of one population were rice growers, while the founding fathers of the other population were wheat growers. Growing rice requires the construction of irrigation systems and the utilization of excess water, as well as work that cannot be done on a purely individual level. On the other hand, growing wheat does not require a similar degree of coordination and cooperation between people. It is more dependent on rainfall and other factors of nature. On the basis of this climatic reality, habits, practices, symbols, and myths were created that were passed down from generation to generation and, in fact, continue to exist even years after the descendants of the rice and wheat growers ceased to engage in their ancestral occupations.

A study conducted at San Francisco International Airport[28] creatively illustrates this argument. The researchers "ambushed" passengers who had landed at the airport and asked them to choose one pencil from a bunch of pencils. All the pencils in the bunch were yellow – except for one, which was green. The travelers who came from Southeast Asia – the more "collectivist" cultures, chose one of the yellow pencils. On the other hand, American (more individualistic) travelers were more likely to choose the green pencil, which stood out from the rest.

We will now summarize the main argument, which will serve to analyze charisma and leadership later in the book. As human beings, we are "surrounded" by signals. Some we ignore, some we respond to after examination and consideration (System 2 thinking), while others we respond to quickly in a way that tends to be described by adjectives like "automatic" or "instinctive" (System 1 thinking). The latter are more anchored in evolutionary origins. Our responses to them were not acquired by any deliberate or dedicated process. Instead, these reactions seem to be an inherent part of human nature, something we are born with, which allows us to essentially respond to signals related to primary needs, such as physical threats. These kinds of signals are characterized as having universal validity.

The signals at the other end of the continuum are those to which responses are clearly acquired in the process of socialization. For example, a "flag" is a (visual) symbol of a group. Whether it is the flag of a football team, a military unit, or a national flag, it is a symbol that contains colors or shapes that make members of a particular group feel a sense of identity and sometimes even excitement. The flag which causes members of one group to get excited does not necessarily cause a similar reaction in people who are not members of this particular group. In fact, they may be completely indifferent to the flag displayed and may not even know which group it represents. However, we will respond to a flag emotionally and quickly (automatic response – System 1) if it is *our* flag. The ability to identify a particular flag as "different", as "unique", compared to other flags, is learned. *But the need for symbols themselves – as creators and strengtheners of group solidarity – is universal.*

Leaders or candidates for leadership positions also serve as "signals". The degree of charisma attributed to these figures, the willingness of others to be led by them, can be understood and interpreted in their analysis as signals. The Rebbe of Lubavitch, who is revered by a certain group of religious Jews, is not a symbol for others, who cannot even understand the charisma attributed to him. This type of admiration can only be experienced in the context of a group culture.

Now, equipped with the evolutionary perspectives and key concepts discussed, we turn to the questions that form the core of this book: Why are we attracted to leaders? Why are we attracted to different types of leaders? Why do we perceive certain leaders as more charismatic than others? Why do some leaders, who are perceived as charismatic during a certain period, stop being perceived as such in another period? Why do some leaders become "eternally charismatic" – beyond time and place, while others fall, forgotten, into the abyss of oblivion? What are the universal components and cultural components that underlie attraction to leaders? In fact, what are the components that make up the multi-layered phenomenon called "followership"?

The "signal model", which will be used later in the book, provides us with conceptual and researchable options to deal with these questions. We will begin the discussion with universal signals relevant to leadership and followership, after which we will analyze these aspects in the context of culturally acquired signals.

NOTES

1. Kafashan, Sara, Sparks, Adam, Rotella, Amanda, and Barclay, Pat (2017). Why heroism exists. Evolutionary perspectives on external helping. In Allison, Scott, George, Goethals, and Roderick M. Kramer (eds), *Handbook of Heroism and Heroic Leadership*. New York: Routledge, pp. 36–58.
2. Kenrick, Douglas T. and Griskevicius, Vladas (2013). *The Rational Animal. How Evolution Made Us Smarter Than We Think*. New York: Basic Books.
3. Kahneman, Daniel and Tversky, Amos (1972). Subjective probability: A judgment of representativeness. *Cognitive Psychology*, 3, 430–54.
4. Lewis, Michael (2016). *The Undoing Project. A Friendship That Changed Our Mind*. New York: Norton.
5. Lakshminarayanan, Venkat M., Chen, Keith, and Santos, Laurie (2008). Endowment effect in Capuchin monkeys. *Philosophical Transactions of the Royal Society B: Biological Sciences*, 363, 3837–44.
6. Kenrick and Griskevicius, *The Rational Animal*.
7. Harari, Yuval N. (2015). *Sapiens: A Brief History of Humankind*. New York: Harper and Collins.
8. Kenrick and Griskevicius, *The Rational Animal*.
9. Kenrick, Douglas T. and Keefe, Richard C. (1992). Age preferences in mates reflect sex differences in human reproductive strategies. *Behavioral and Brain Sciences*, 15, 75–133. Buss, David (1989). Sex differences in human mate preferences: Evolutionary hypotheses tested in 37 cultures. *Behavioral and Brain Sciences*, 12, 1–49.
10. Kenrick, Douglas T., Keefe, Richard C., Bryan, Angella, Barr, Alicia, and Brown, Stephanie (1995). Age preferences and mate choice among heterosexuals: A case for modular psychological mechanisms. *Journal of Personality and Social Psychology*, 69, 1166–72.
11. Zahavi, Amotz and Zahavi, Avishag (1997). *The Handicap Principle: A Missing Piece of Darwin's Puzzle*. New York: Oxford University Press.
12. Zajonc, Robert (1980). Feeling and thinking. Preferences need no inferences. *American Psychologist*, 35(2), 151–75.
13. LoBue, V. and DeLoach, J.S. (2008). Detecting a snake in the grass: Attention to fear-relevant stimuli by adults and young children. *Psychological Science*, 19(3), 284–9.
14. Lampert. Ada (1997). *The Evolution of Love*. Westport, CT: Praeger.
15. Kahneman. Daniel (2011). *Thinking Fast and Slow*. New York: Farrar, Straus and Giroux.
16. Haldane, John Burdon (1935). *The Philosophy of a Biologist*. Oxford: Clarendon Press.
17. Fisher, Ronald A. (1930). *The General Theory of Natural Selection*. Cambridge: Cambridge University Press.
18. Emerson, Alfred (1946). The biological basis of social cooperation. *Illinois Academy of Science Transactions*, 39, 12.
19. Harman, Oren (2011). *The Price of Altruism and the Search for the Origins of Kindness*. New York: Norton.

20. Waal, Frans B.M. de (1996). *Good Natured*. Cambridge, MA: Harvard University Press.
21. Derks, Bella, Sheepers, Daan, and Ellemers, Naomi (eds) (2013). *Neuroscience of Prejudice and Intergroup Relations*. New York: Psychology Press.
22. Buttelmann, David, Zmyj, Norbert, Daum, Moritz, and Carpenter, Malinda (2013). Selective imitation of in-group over out-group members in 14-month-old infants. *Child Development*, 84(2), 422–8.
23. Disendruck, Gil and Weiss, Eitan (2015). Differential weighting of cues to social categories. *Cognitive Development*, 33, 56–72.
24. Harari, *Sapiens*.
25. Haldane, John. Burdon. (1935). *The Philosophy of a Biologist*. Oxford: Clarendon Press.
26. Tallhelm, Thomas., Zhang, Xuemin., Oishi, Shige., Shimin, Chen., Duan, Dchao., Lan, Xiali. and Kitayama, Shinobu. (2014). Large-scale psychological differences within China explained by rice versus wheat agriculture. *Science*, 344(6184), 603–608.
27. Hofstede, Geert and Hofstede, Jan. (2005). *Culture and Organizations: The Software of the Mind*, New York: McGraw-Hill.
28. Kim, Heejung and Markus, Hazel, R. (1999). Deviance or uniqueness, harmony or conformity? A cultural analysis. *Journal of Personality and Social Psychology*, 77, 4, 785–800.

3. The attraction to leaders

When Israeli Prime Minister, Yitzhak Rabin, was assassinated in November 1995 in Kings of Israel Square (now called Rabin Square) in Tel Aviv, countless people wept and grieved. There was a particularly prominent emotional reaction to the youth who lit candles in the square and cried: "Our father has been killed."

The spontaneous and authentic link that these young people made on the night of the murder – between a leader and a father figure – has been extensively discussed in the psychological literature, especially in the psychoanalytic streams[1] dealing with the inner emotional unconscious worlds of human beings. Metaphorically, the psychoanalytic claim is that some of our most disturbing, painful, and anxious emotions are repressed and kept "locked away in the basement". When they somehow manage to break out, they are often associated with basic feelings such as the fear of abandonment, or helplessness that played a central role in the individual's early life.

The idea that our "unconscious" parts have weight and influence our reactions and decisions is common knowledge today. This is clearly evident in numerous aspects of the Western world: from the interpretation of myths, through plays, books, films, poetry, and research. However, when this notion was first introduced by Freud in 1896, it was criticized mainly because, in the eyes of the critics, it was considered "unscientific", "unobservable", and "unmeasurable".

From a historical point of view, it may not be a theoretical discussion; but, in some respects, it may be interpreted as a technical issue. Although many tend to forget this fact, Freud was a neurologist. As such, he first examined the physiological sources of symptomatic phenomena. The mental leap that led him to psychoanalytic interpretations was actually due to his inability as a physician to find the physiological source of distress in one of his patients. Thus, his investigation into the "origins of distress" led him to the now long-accepted link between psychological and physiological processes.

Today's technology allows us to identify and diagnose brain activity which indicates emotions; emotions such as fear, aggression, and empathy can be classified according to brain correlates.[2] Due to these developments, it is currently possible from a historical viewpoint to interpret Freud's contribution as a clinical insight that connects body and mind, without having the technological means to observe and detect such a connection.

The person who pointed out this connection emphatically was John Bowlby, a British psychiatrist who formulated the *attachment theory*,[3] which has had a huge theoretical impact and serves as the basis for thousands of studies in developmental and social psychology. It would not be an exaggeration to state that attachment theory is one of the most influential theories in the history of psychology. In fact, it is one of the relatively few psychological theories based on evolutionary premises, shifting to a great extent, the emphasis from unconscious mental motives and impulses to the idea of active adaptation to the environment. This theory is important in relation to the subjects discussed in this book for several reasons. First, it demonstrates a form of psychological thinking that stems from evolutionary observation. In addition, the studies conducted on the basis of the theory well illustrate the idea of signals triggering reactions of emotional origin. Finally, it clarifies the centrality of "large figures" in human life.

"Large figures" is a generic title for parents, teachers, counselors, and other authoritative figures who we "look up to". We argue that leaders are part of this general category. That is, in order to understand the role of leaders in our lives, we must understand the emotions aroused in us by primary "large figures" in our lives. This is a central and well-known claim in psychoanalytic thought.

Indeed, psychoanalysts who have dealt with leadership have perceived the dynamics with parental figures as key to understanding the attraction to leaders; as well as to some people's desire to be in leadership roles. (A well-known example of a psychoanalytic discussion of motivation to lead is presented in Eric Erickson's book.[4]) Bowlby's thought confers a different epistemic status to the "large figure": a status that is beyond the specific relationship dynamics that a particular person had with his parents and family members. The large figure has, first and foremost, an evolutionary role: to enable the biological existence of the baby. It all starts with this initial fact. We will now address the meanings that emerge from this perspective.

UNIVERSAL SIGNS OF LEADERSHIP

As stated, the origins of attachment theory are biological-evolutionary. Most animals know how to run, fly, hide – in order to maintain their survival during the very early stages of life. The human baby cannot survive even a few days without the care of a "large figure", who feeds him, cleans him, and protects him – from the cold, the heat, or the threat of "suspicious figures". Hence, the initial affinity to large figures is rooted in an existential need. Indeed, the connection to the large figure (the "caring figure" – in many cases – the mother) is made at this stage which is pre-verbal, by means of *signals*. When the baby is hungry, thirsty, cold, or uncomfortable because he needs to have his diaper changed, he will display signs such as crying or murmurs that draw the caregiver's attention to his distress. This caregiver is supposed to be equipped with the necessary sensitivity required to respond to the baby's signals.

So far, nothing new has been said. However, Bowlby's great contribution was in illuminating the emotional significance of this period later in life. Although the affinity between the baby and the large figure is rooted in fundamental existential needs, in the case of humans – which is unique – the *way* in which the primary needs are met affects the individual's lifelong emotional development. If the large figure is responsive to the baby's distress signals by being available, consistent and relevant, then the infant, in his initial contact, learns that he is "in good hands". This leads the baby to create an "internal working model", which is based on trust (a secure attachment pattern). On the other hand, if the caregiver's responses are inconsistent or irrelevant to the baby's needs, the infant will develop insecure attachment patterns (there are different types of insecure patterns derived from different types of caregiver responsiveness).[5]

Bowlby's groundbreaking argument was that the patterns formed in infancy will be reflected in emotional relationships in adulthood. Thus, for example, differences in responses were found between the secure and insecure attachment patterns in the quality of romantic relationships,[6] in reference to friends,[7] and also (as we will explain below), in reference to leaders and followers.[8]

However, the most central aspect of our discussion, which is at the basis of attachment theory and is often taken for granted, is the inherent longing of humans for a large figure that will provide them with a sense of security. Bowlby interpreted this as an inherent and existential longing for the "strong and the wise".[9]

Indeed, as noted, this motif is interpreted in psychoanalytic thinking as a longing for the parent figure. For example, the psychoanalyst, Melvin Hill, demonstrated this argument in a simple semantic analysis. In descriptions of people perceived as fulfilling leadership roles, Hill identified a copious degree of "parental expressions".[10]

The term "father", for example, frequently appears in reference to representations of authority. Although there is a "technical" word for pastor, many churchgoers call the pastor "father". Even teachers and educators, when considered meaningful, are often described as "spiritual fathers or mothers". Leaders perceived by the public as founders of a given collective – be it a state, a community, or an organization – are called "the nation's father", "the community's father", and so on. In prayers and supplications, people refer to God as "our Father in heaven", while supporting and benevolent women are often called "mothers" (e.g., Mother Theresa).

This inherent longing for a strong, protective figure, signifying: "You can relax", was well described by Eleanor Roosevelt (Franklin Roosevelt's wife) after Franklin Roosevelt's inauguration as President of the United States, which took place in the midst of the Great Depression: "When Franklin said in his inauguration speech that he might have to assume presidential powers that are usually assumed by the president in wartime, just in that part of the speech he received the most thunderous applause."[11]

Indeed, most prominent and decisive manifestations of the longing for a protective figure are expressed by people during what they perceive as crisis situations concerning their primary needs. The most prominent historical example of this argument is probably that of Adolf Hitler. In the hundreds of attempts to decipher the riddle of his rise to a leadership position, the most agreed-upon explanation is the psychological effect of the terrible economic and social crisis in Germany between the two world wars. Studies have indeed shown that many of the most charismatic leaders in history have emerged on the waves of crises.[12]

Thus, the first type of signal indicating "Who deserves to lead?" is the sign that Bowlby referred to as signifying the existence of "power and wisdom". That is, signals that radiate "competence regarding what needs to be done" – "knowing how to deal with difficulties". The evolutionary element of such a signal is clearly observed among animals living in groups. The group members will let the most powerful (competent) animal lead them.[13] The parallel example of this among humans is not necessarily a physical force, but rather a competence that has a clear existential value. Thus, our forefathers allowed the individual whom they perceived as capable of finding water sources to lead them. In other words, the first signal that prompts us to be led by a leader is a "signal of competence".

In an experiment conducted at Princeton University, Todorov and colleagues[14] presented students with facial photographs of men for short periods of time up to a second, and then asked them to rate the face according to various traits, one of which was "competence" – the ability to solve problems in a relevant context.

The faces presented were not a random sample – they were all portraits from election campaigns. Todorov and colleagues compared the election results in the various states to the ratings of the Princeton students, which were based on brief exposure with no previous recognition by the students. In 70 percent of the races for senator, congressman, or governor the winner of the election was the candidate whose face was ranked higher in terms of competence by the students (the researchers examined the possibility of a "halo effect", which can significantly "paint" a perception of other traits, e.g., good looks).

The study indicated that the perception of competence was the most significant variable in the prediction. This impressive result has been confirmed in elections to regional councils in Finland, England, and in various election races in Australia, Germany, and Mexico.[15]

Antonakis and Dalgas from the University of Lausanne[16] provided additional support to the claim that reactions to certain signals are innate. In an experiment they conducted, the methodology of Todorov and colleagues was repeated, but this time the subjects were children between the ages of 5 and 13, who were clearly less experienced and more naive in their judgments (i.e., they had fewer "political considerations"). The researchers presented the children with pictures of politicians on the pretext that they should choose team leaders for a hypothetical game. The children's pattern of choice was the same as that of the adults reported by Todorov and his colleagues in their research – fast, instinctive, and based on the sense of competence inferred from the pictures.

This insight is very important in our attempt to decipher initial instincts in choosing a leader. One of the most prominent and clear situations that can help us elaborate on these questions is *an election campaign.* If we look at the campaigns of political leaders as a psycho-social experiment in which people (especially those who run for the first time) try to convince thousands – sometimes millions – of people regardless of age, gender, or religion that they are best suited to lead them, we can better understand the nature of the signals that "signify" alleged leadership.

A thought-provoking historical example of the centrality of "evolutionary signals" in election campaigns was raised by Malcolm Gladwell,[17] describing the process of electing Warren Harding as President of the United States.

The idea to have Harding run for the US presidential election was born at a meeting one day in 1899, in which two people met by chance while their shoes were being brushed and polished on the porch of the Richwood Ohio Hotel. One of them was Harry Daugherty, a shrewd and brilliant lawyer who was considered a local Machiavellian politician. The other individual was Warren Harding, a newspaper editor in the town of Marion, who was about to be elected senator of the state. Daugherty took one glance at Harding and quickly concluded: We (the Republicans) have an excellent candidate here for the presidency of the United States.

How was this decision made so quickly? Journalist Mark Sullivan's description provides an answer: "[Harding's] appearance is more than the adjective 'good looking' implies. He looks 'Roman'" (as he was later called). His biographer, Francis Russel, noted that if Harding had worn a robe, he could easily have played the character of Julius Caesar in the play. His broad shoulders, his height, his gray hair, his face as if formed in bronze, the way he walked, his thunderous voice – all collaborated to make him a man who makes a huge impression. Indeed, Daugherty, the experienced Machiavellian, was convinced. At the party convention in Chicago, many wondered: Who looks more "presidential" than Harding? And indeed, Harding was elected as the party's candidate and later elected President of the United States.

A wonderful and sarcastic example of the impact of such signals, especially in situations of uncertainty, was given in a book that focused on the "psychology of the followers",[18] in which an example taken from the book written by the Polish-American author Jersey Kosinski, *Being There*,[19] was presented and analyzed.

In the book, Kosinski describes how Chauncey – a simple, middle-aged gardener with learning difficulties, who worked all his life on an old man's estate, dividing his time between gardening and watching silly TV shows – is forced to leave the mansion, after his benefactor dies. While walking for the first time in the city's tumultuous streets, he is slightly injured by a passing limousine. The passenger, Mrs. Rand, the wife of the chairman of a huge American corporation, decides to take him home to make sure he is unharmed. In a conversation between them, she is deeply impressed by the "rare intelligence and insight", as she puts it, that Chauncey possesses. In fact, in his conversations with Mrs. Rand the gardener simply does what he learned from the TV shows he watched: he repeats her words in an empathetic tone.

Mrs. Rand is not the only one who is impressed. Her husband, too, is deeply impressed by the gardener's "wisdom". When Mr. Rand asks him about his business, the conversation between them is as follows: "It's not easy, sir," Chauncey replies, "there are not many options to get to a good garden, where you can work without interruption, and grow there according to the changing seasons." Mr. Rand, who is sure that Chauncey is using a metaphor to describe the crisis in the US economy, responds enthusiastically: "Garden, huh? Wonderful wording! Isn't this a wonderful and accurate description of a real businessman? Yes, Chauncey, what a wonderful metaphor! Indeed, a productive businessman is like a farmer cultivating his garden."

When the President of the United States, who consults with businessman Rand, asks Chauncey about the country's economic difficulties, Chauncey replies: "There are always seasons in gardening: there is spring, there is summer, but there is also winter and autumn, and then again spring and summer. As long as the roots are not seriously damaged, everything is fine." The President of the United States is deeply impressed and adopts the gardener's "seasons" metaphor in his speeches.

Chauncey's career develops rapidly. He is invited to appear on an important TV show. In the opening, the interviewer notes that the President of the United States has compared the American economy to a garden. Chauncey, given permission to speak, speaks of the only thing he knows: "I know the garden well," he says emphatically, "I have worked in this occupation all my life. The garden is good and healthy, the trees are healthy and so are the flowers and other vegetation. I agree with the words of the President of the United States. There is room for new trees and new flowers of various kinds."

The audience responds enthusiastically to Chauncey's "profound" words. When asked by reporters which newspapers he prefers to read, Chauncey replies that he does not read any newspaper (he is illiterate): "I compulsively watch TV shows." His answer is accepted as one of the sincerest statements a public figure has ever made. Chauncey becomes a public darling, is voted the most "elegant man", and all the newspapers want to publish cover stories about him. And so it goes, until Chauncey, the simple gardener, is elected as a presidential candidate.

Kosinski's Chauncey expresses the need humans have to create great figures for themselves – even when the object of admiration is a completely empty vessel. Chauncey's meticulous dress, dignified gray hair, courtly manners, and above all, his calm expression (he did not understand what was wanted of him), which were perceived by the public as great composure, self-control, and the supreme ability to handle crisis situations, strengthened his image as a worthy leader.

The studies of Todorov, Antonakis, and their colleagues suggest that the aforementioned examples are not "satirical literary", but rather demonstrate the idea of "signals". The more instinctive signals (System 1) – which signify that a certain figure is worthy to lead – are physical: size, facial expressions, and height. Then come features such as a deep voice, decisive tone, and other characteristics that always add points to the leadership image.[20]

Finally, there are invisible "informative clues" (e.g., degrees from prestigious institutions), which seemingly attest to competence, which clearly enhance the candidate's image as a leader. If we rank the degree of effectiveness in empowering candidates for leadership positions, we can see what shrewd advertisers who specialize in election campaigns know very well: how to influence the public's emotions in the most effective way. Regarding human emotion, focusing on the longing for security is very effective, while addressing or generating existential fear are the strongest of all – as evidenced by the cynical statement of Nazi leader, Herman Goering: "You can always get people to follow leaders. It's easy. All you have to say is that they are being attacked."[21]

Israel is a prominent, and perhaps unique, example in the West of illustrating this claim. This is because of the public feeling that the existence of the State is not guaranteed. Indeed, the "security signal" has had enormous value in the history of the country's political elections. In the terms presented, signals perceived by the public as indicating relevant abilities to deal with threatening environments were of high electoral value. The fact that the Israeli political leadership throughout the years of the State's existence includes so many generals and heads of security agencies cannot be seen as coincidental. In Western countries where the sense of threat is not intensely experienced by the public, there is no such high value for signals of this kind.[22]

Ariel Sharon's campaign to become Israel's prime minister illustrates this argument very well. Sharon was portrayed as a "strong man", who could deal well with existential dangers. His pictures as a general and stories about his ability to function well in wartime were repeatedly highlighted. However, it seems that the managers of Sharon's campaign felt there was another emotion that would have a particularly strong effect on voters: human warmth. They rightly felt the centrality of this emotion in human experience – a claim that has been supported by both evolutionary researchers and social psychologists.

For example, in one social psychology experiment, the researcher gave the subjects a list of traits of two people who were completely identical in their characteristics (e.g., they were identical in height) The only trait that was different was in relation to the "warmth" dimension: one individual was portrayed as "warm" and the other was portrayed as "cold". Subjects were asked to describe the two people. It turned out that the "warmth factor" had a "halo effect", meaning, it impacted on the subject's perception regarding all of the other personality traits. The "warm" person was described by the subjects as scoring higher on all of the characteristics.[23]

Thus, it is seemingly not accidental that campaign managers urge their clients to take pictures with babies and shake hands in markets – gestures that are perceived as showing "human warmth". Even before the official start of the Trump campaign (when most commentators and journalists assumed that Hillary Clinton's victory was guaranteed and decisive), Trump's campaign manager, Steve Bannon, claimed that Trump had a good chance of winning because Hillary Clinton's messages were conveyed to the public as if "read by a machine" – meaning Clinton was perceived as a cold person.[24]

In retrospect, it turned out that the "warmth factor" was a better (though not the sole) predictor of success than Hillary Clinton's impressive career in a variety of public service roles. "Warmth" is a sort of evolutionary signal, which signifies "care". As mentioned, the primacy of care signals was reported in a study on forest animals.[25] The animals followed the animal which they sensed to be the best protector (the best fighter). However, if the leading animal did not share the prey with the other group members, not only did they stop following him/her, they might even kill him/her. Fiske, Cuddy, and Glick[26] found that competence and warmth have a definite prominence in interpersonal relationships. The reasons for this were interpreted by them as evolutionary – these are the first signals that signify "permission" to grant trust. "Trust" is a central pillar in human development. "Mistakes" regarding the granting of trust might have been crucial in terms of survival.

The examples presented highlight the fragility of the leadership signals displayed in an election campaign. History points to many instances where there have been gaps between "promised" leadership and "actual" leadership. Had the "Roman-looking" President, Warren Harding, been investigated thoroughly before the campaign, a wealth of evidence – both regarding his superficiality and his motives – would have been revealed. In his service in the Senate, Harding was not involved in the most important political debates of the period: women's suffrage and the prohibition of alcoholic beverages. In fact, he was not even personally motivated to be President of the United States. Those who pushed him to do so were his wife Florence and, of course, Dougherty and the political apparatus he represented. After two years of presidency, Harding suffered a stroke and died. Historians rank him as one of the worst presidents in American history.[27]

These gaps between signals in an election campaign and actual functioning as a leader over time are primarily due to the inability during campaigns to truly validate the credibility of such signals. In order to test the reliability of these signals (even for the purpose of a conceptual discussion), we must refer to the distance of followers from their leader as amplifying biases in information processing.[28] We must also take the circumstances into account. As we have seen, circumstances of severe uncertainty create a sense of threat that somewhat resembles the constant feelings of early *Homo sapiens*.

In thousands of studies – in fact, most of the empirical work on leadership – the distance from the leader is limited. The studies were conducted in organizations, communities, and groups in which the subjects usually met their leaders directly and were able to observe their daily behaviors.[29] In many of these studies, the researchers used a questionnaire called the MLQ – multi-factor leadership questionnaire, which is the most commonly used questionnaire in leadership research. The questionnaire is based on the responses of many people from different fields to two questions: (a) Who influenced you? and (b) What was it about them that made an impact? According to the responses, the researchers came up with a list of influential behaviors. This list has undergone statistical validation using a technique known as *factor analysis*. These factors (nine in all, which make up the questionnaire) measure the effect of influence as it is perceived by the followers.[30]

The factor that has the most weight – about two-thirds of the effect – is called "idealized influence". Examining the items that make up this factor shows that the most influential component inherent in this factor can be related to "personal example". The leader's observed behaviors apparently inspire followers more than any other element.

In the discussed evolutionary terms, the place where this finding is probably most obvious is in combat situations in the military service framework. Combat service conditions are the closest simulation in our modern age to an encounter that reflects the most basic/primal feelings of existential struggle. Therefore, analyzing leadership signals in this context can provide us with more relevant insights compared to other environments where the existential threat is less present in the minds of the people.

Indeed, findings of studies dealing with military leadership point to the centrality of *trust in commanders* as the most important variable in troops' willingness to go into battle.[31] Moreover, a lack of trust in commanders can be devastating. For example, in their book on the Vietnam War, Richard Gabriel and Paul Savage reported 800 cases of "intentional harm" to junior commanders between 1969 and 1972 as a result of mistrust, which in some extreme cases led to assassination.[32]

How do soldiers decide that their commanders (whom they perceive as "large figures") deserve their trust in the "purest" test of all – the existential test? The findings clearly show the same signals discussed in the literature review presented in the previous chapter: (a) competence (the commanders' professionalism) and (b) caring. However, unlike election campaigns, soldiers have the opportunity to test the reliability of these signals. They can examine, in a much more meticulous and reliable way, whether these signals are true, a bias of information processing, or simply manipulation.

The main concept for examining this issue (which the combat service scenario provides, as mentioned, with more "prominent" laboratory conditions) is *price*. The argument is that the higher the price paid by the large figure, the greater the credibility of the signals is in the eyes of the followers (we saw this in the example of the peacock's tail in the previous chapter – the handicap principle). The price has more to do with the caring signals because they can be faked more easily. It is more difficult to identify whether the handshakes, the hugs in the markets, the kissing of babies, and the pats on the back of politicians are real manifestations of warmth or whether they are merely "staged expressions" required under the circumstances of an election campaign. Indeed, the issue of *authenticity* has become central to leadership research.[33]

We will now summarize what has been said in this chapter. From the point of view of the followers, leadership has signals. These signals trigger feelings and reactions. The clearest responses to leaders (and candidates for leadership positions) are those that have roots in the phylogeny of *Homo sapiens*. The main signals are competence and warmth (caring). When these signals are experienced, the followers tend to place great trust in the leader.

However, inherent in this explanation is also a "trap" associated with the signals' degree of proven reliability (authenticity). These signals, especially signals of warmth and caring, can be misleading. They are more prone to bias and even manipulation, especially in circumstances of distance from the leader (such as in election campaigns) or in the absence of a sense of dealing with adaptive challenges. In other words, the question of the validity of trust in a leader is complex and multifaceted. It is simpler to validate the credibility of a company commander's leadership compared to that of a political leader, especially one who strives for leadership positions in an election campaign. What are the theoretical and psychological implications of this issue? Can they be dealt with? We will discuss this again after presenting the acquired cultural signals associated with leadership.

CULTURAL SIGNALS OF LEADERSHIP

Captain Wolfgen Hoffman was an ardent murderer of Jews. As commander of one of the three companies in the 101st Police Battalion, he led, like his fellow officers, his subordinates – who were not SS men, but ordinary Germans – the deportation and horrific massacre of tens of thousands of Jewish men, women, and children in Poland. On one occasion, however, in the midst of his genocidal activities, this man openly refused to obey the order of his superiors because he believed the order was immoral. The ordinance instructed Hoffman's men to sign a routine statement pledging not to steal or accept anything they hadn't paid for (i.e., bribes). In the opening of Hoffman's letter of refusal to sign, he says that upon first reading the order, he thought a mistake had been made: "since I thought it was first-degree impudence to demand that a decent German soldier sign a statement pledging not to steal or accept anything he hadn't paid for ...".

He went on and clarified that this demand was unnecessary, since his people, imbued with proper ideological beliefs, were well aware that such behavior was inappropriate. He even told his superiors his opinion on the nature of his subordinates and their actions, including, presumably, the massacres they committed against the Jews. He wrote that his men's "adherence to German norms of morality and conduct stems from free will, not from the pursuit of benefits or fear of punishment". Hoffman then defiantly declared: "As an officer, I am sorry that my opinion is contrary to that of the battalion commander and that I am unable to carry out the order. As I feel that my honor has been violated, I must refuse to sign this general declaration."

This event opens historian, Daniel Jonah Goldhagen's, book *Ordinary Germans and the Holocaust*,[34] which was a prominent milestone in Holocaust research, since it was an original analysis that dealt with both the perpetrators and the victims.

Officer Hoffman's letter, according to Goldhagen, is very instructive since by the time he wrote it he had already led his men in the massacre of tens of thousands of Jews, but he still thought it was impudent to imagine that he and his men were capable of stealing from the Poles or taking bribes. Apparently, Hoffman attributed to the organization in which he served enough tolerance to risk a written refusal of a direct command. This letter indicates that the murder of Jewish men, women, and children was not an issue whose morality must be challenged.

The thought of murdering Jews did not concern Hoffman and his men at all. This is the uniqueness, according to Goldhagen, of German anti-Semitism during the Holocaust. It was, by definition, "eliminative anti-Semitism", and thus different and unique compared to the "ordinary" anti-Semitism which had been carried out in Europe for centuries.

The interesting point of this report is the argument that eliminative anti-Semitism was a German cultural phenomenon. This is seemingly a very extreme example. However, only extreme examples can clearly magnify those phenomena that are more difficult to distinguish through common observations.

Moreover, it is assumed that cultural anthropologists should ignore prototypical concepts or inclusive theses such as "national character". The research approach to culture requires observing behaviors that are systematic, and trying to deduce the thought patterns shared by a given group.

This was the approach that guided Goldhagen. He simply examined patterns of thinking and behaviors of "ordinary Germans" during the war. Based on the collected data, he understood that eliminative anti-Semitism is linked to culture.

This is, therefore, a test case ("magnified" as aforesaid) for a form of thinking and analysis regarding the so-called obscure concept which we refer to as "culture". Our basic argument is that the more people in a given collective think and behave in a certain way – in a distinct pattern – the more it expresses a "cultural pattern".

Using this approach, the behavior of soldiers and officers in the 101st Police Battalion, which operated from June 1942 to early 1944 in the Lublin district, was analyzed. The choice of this unit was not accidental, since it is a unit that actually served as a police force. Its members had not previously served in any military or security institution; therefore, it was reasonable to assume that they were not endowed with a particularly militant spirit or temperament.

The unit numbered about 500 men. Their average age was 36.5 years, when they began their murderous operations. Only 42 of them were under the age of 30, 153 were over 40, and 9 were over the age of 50. Nearly three-quarters (73.6 percent) were born between 1900 and 1909; that is, were considered too old for military combat service.

In short, these were experienced, mature men who had families and children, and who for the most part had reached adulthood before Nazism came to power. A total of 180 of these men were middle-class civil servants and traders, while 291 were senior managers and public servants. Unskilled peasants or workers were the minority. Their age, background (mostly urban), and the distribution of their occupations also make it very clear that this group of men is indeed representative of "ordinary Germans". These "ordinary Germans" committed murders that are hard to describe, and they were not committed during a battle on the front lines, but in towns where their unit had a police station.

Why is this considered a case indicating a cultural aspect? It is the common everyday discourse and the repetitive behaviors that attest to this perhaps most clearly of all. For example, the wife of a battalion officer who had come to stay with her husband in one of the towns said: "One morning, I was eating with my husband in the garden of the building where he lived, when a simple policeman from his platoon approached us, saluted, and announced: "Sir, I have not eaten breakfast yet." When asked why, he continued: "I have not yet murdered any Jews [today]."[35]

Countless articles and books have attempted to decipher the reasons for the Nazis' murder of Jews. World War II was not the first war to produce unimaginable manifestations of violence. The unique point regarding World War II is the attempt to systematically eliminate a certain group without being able to identify any existential threats to the attackers, no territorial struggle, no struggle for resources or interests, not even a struggle for narrative or respect of any kind, which can be found at the foundation of wars throughout history. In the case of World War II, the Germans murdered – on a large scale and systematically, with machine guns, mass graves, and the efficient management of extermination camps – millions of men, women, and children, including the elderly, who obviously could not have instigated a reason for their murder.

The explanation for this unique phenomenon according to Goldhagen is, as stated, cultural, and a confirmation of this argument is the absence of any guilt feelings in the exterminators – the "ordinary people". The cultural aspect whose origins are also theological in this case gave the Jews the status of cockroaches. This is, in a sense, an aesthetic claim. You eliminate cockroaches without undue thought and immediately return to your usual occupations. They are dirty, unpleasant creatures that taint the environment – an "annoyance", which one gets rid of. It is a fact that the "ordinary Germans" of Battalion 101 did not treat other groups in the occupied territories in the cruel, destructive, and remorseless manner in which they treated the Jews.

According to Goldhagen, the Jews were eliminated by Battalion 101 beyond any order and beyond the perception of an enemy as a threat in a war between armies and peoples. This was done willingly and even enthusiastically, similar perhaps to someone who weeds his garden of dirt so that it will look better.

The perception of the Jew as a disgusting creature is a cultural aspect that has been passed down from generation to generation. It has been integrated into German culture and absorbed in socialization processes such as love of music and other aesthetic aspects. The point that allows interpretation in this direction stems from the lack of remorse. The 101st Battalion did not act out of uncontrolled anger or fear of threat. Their behavior is characterized by composure, a sense of distance, and complete control of their instincts. In the eyes of many Germans, Jews had the status of dirt, which necessarily needed to be removed in a practical manner and, as mentioned: without any guilt feelings.

In his book on the history of German Jews, Amos Elon[36] describes their lives in Germany and how they resided there for hundreds of years. At the very beginning of the book a description, which has a symbolic meaning indicating a cultural reference to the Jews, is presented. The book describes that there were gates in the wall surrounding the city, which were intended for animals only. Jews were only allowed to enter the city through these gates. Thus, their status was similar to that of the pigs who entered through the same gates. Both were filthy, ugly and belonged to other, inhuman, categories. Whatever their title may have been, they were not perceived as humans who deserved to be treated with respect and equality.

It is also possible that the word "hatred", although widely used in this context, is simply inappropriate, as it describes an emotion that is very strong and focused. The word "disgust" more appropriately befits the indifference Germans expressed toward children's lives simply because they were Jews. There was no cultural upheaval in Nazi Germany. A more accurate interpretation would be to perceive this collective behavior in Germany as a unique combination (in the historical sense) of dormant "cultural emotions" and a one-time cruel and murderous regime.

It should be emphasized that we are not dealing here with another claim concerning the study of the Holocaust. As stated, we present this extreme context in order to highlight the meaning of "culture", in terms of the subconscious patterns and behaviors resulting from it. (We stress the fact that there is no intention here to determine "German nature". To be precise, Goldhagen himself does not claim that his analysis is relevant to today's German population. According to his impression, the trauma of the war led to a substantial change process in German culture.)

What distinguished the events that occurred in Nazi Germany is described by leadership scholars by using the metaphor of "fire".[37] Fire is a product of three factors: (1) the spark, which serves to ignite combustibles (the leader); (2) combustible materials (the followers); and (3) the oxygen that feeds the fire (circumstances). In Nazi Germany, these three factors were uniquely intertwined. Had it not been for the circumstances of such a terrible economic, social, and psychological crisis between the two world wars, the spark (Hitler) might not have been chosen and ignited the combustibles (the German people), which were soaked in a substance that was particularly flammable (the crisis situation). The claim we make (illustrated above) pertains to "combustibles" and leadership. The argument is that some responses are triggered by signals that are culturally anchored.

Followers, as analyzed in the previous chapter, can be triggered by signals. Such signals can be *universal and imprinted or cultural and learned* (e.g., anthem, a flag, etc.). Cultural/learned signals trigger reactions that are unique to a particular group. As such, they will not necessarily trigger the same level of intensity (or any reaction at all) in another group. If we use the image presented above – these are examples of combustibles with different sensitivities.

True, the claim presented through the example of Nazi Germany can be criticized as being unique to a certain period in history, and "too political" to be used as a generalization. However, we emphasize that there is no exceptional research approach here. In both the world of medicine and the world of clinical psychology, it is customary to take the more differentiated, sometimes pathological cases, in order to investigate a phenomenon in depth. In any case, we will also address the impact of culture within more common patterns of routine life in communities, which can be observed in everyday life, rather than in particularly dramatic historical circumstances.

In the Middle East and Arab countries, there is a specific type of murder that takes place among the Arab population, which has a "cultural label": the murder of women as a manifestation of "family honor". The tag "cultural" in this case is given by the killers themselves and their families. According to them, a woman suspected of infidelity or engaging in any form of forbidden sex casts disgrace upon her family. Therefore, she must be killed. This death sentence is "impersonal"; it is a cultural order, a community order that must be accepted – not only with understanding, but as a proper act in light of the circumstances.

Indeed, the fact that the murderers in many of these cases do not act out of rage or jealousy is evident. Many times, the perpetrators are brothers or fathers of the victim who, according to countless testimonies, loved the sister or daughter deeply. Their reactions testify to the cultural motif. The brother or father feels that he must do the deed in order to "save the honor of the family". Indeed, many phenomena, which are seemingly incomprehensible to Western sensibilities (such as that of someone who kills his sister), take on a different logic when analyzed from a cultural point of view.

An example showing a similar cultural motif was presented by the journalist, Hooding Carter, who lived in the southern part of the United States. He reported his experience as a jury participant:

> The case brought before the jury involved a man who lived next door to a gas station. For several months, he had been the target of various pranks committed by workers and various punks walking around the station. One morning, he emptied his two rifle butts into his tormentors, killing one and injuring another. ... When the jury returned to the astonished judge, Carter was the only juror to cast a vote of "guilty". As one of the other jurors put it, "He (the man on trial) would not have been considered a man if he hadn't shot those guys."[38]

The inference that this is a cultural aspect stems from the fact that jury members are always elected on the basis of being ordinary citizens with no criminal record and who, for the most part, are respectable people in their community. It would not be an exaggeration to assume that such a verdict in the exact same case would not have had identical results had the jurors hailed from Boston – located in the northern part of the United States, and known as being liberal.

Indeed, an experiment conducted by two psychologists on exactly this point demonstrates the weight of the cultural component in people's responses. The researchers examined culture-biased responses through manipulation of an insult.[39]

The first experiment was conducted as follows. In the basement of the University of Michigan Social Sciences building, there is a long, narrow corridor, with filing cabinets on either side. Students were invited, one by one, to enter the classroom and were asked to fill out a questionnaire. They were then told to hand in the questionnaire at the end of the hall and return to the classroom. For half the students (the control group), this was the end of the experiment. The other half were put in a "trap". As they walked down the hall with the questionnaire, a man – a collaborator in the experiment – caught up with them and opened a drawer of one of the filing cabinets. The narrow corridor now became even narrower. As the subject tried to push by and pass him, the collaborator looked up in disgust. He slammed the filing drawer shut, bumped into the participant's shoulder and muttered: "asshole". The researchers wanted to measure the subjects' level of anger. They took saliva samples from students before and after the insult to see if the word "asshole" caused an increase in testosterone and cortisol levels – hormones that trigger arousal and aggression. In addition, they asked the students to read the following story and add to it: "Twenty minutes after arriving at the party, Jill pulled Steve aside and looked upset. 'What happened?' Steve asked. 'This is Larry. He knows you and I are engaged, but he tried to flirt with me twice tonight ...'."

The results of the experiment were unequivocal. There were clear differences in the way the young people responded to the insult. For some, the insult changed their behavior; for others, it did not. The emotional factor that determined how they reacted was not their emotional confidence, their physical appearance, or intellectual differences. What determined it was their *origin*.

Most young people from the northern part of the United States treated the incident with humor. They dismissed it with a laugh. Their testosterone and cortisol levels did not rise. A few of them imagined Steve responding violently to Larry. On the other hand, the southerners were furious. Their cortisol and testosterone levels soared. In the endings they added to the story, Steve pounced on Larry like a lion.

It seems that the idea of a "culture of honor" is not uniquely found among certain Muslim groups. It can also be found in a country like the United States, which is perceived as a developed Western country. Some researchers have tried to characterize the origins and patterns of the "culture of honor" and found that such cultures tend to take root in arid areas where agriculture cannot be practiced. The farmer is less afraid than the shepherd that his livelihood will be stolen. Therefore, the shepherd must make it clear that he is not weak. He must be willing to fight in response to any challenge. This is a world where a person's reputation is at the center of his or her livelihood and self-worth.

This aspect is reflected very clearly in Hollywood's Western movies. The essential motif in these films is the courage and strength of the cowboy, who succeeds in protecting his property. Anthropologist, John Campbell, who studied the cultures of the shepherds in Greece, points to "formative points" in the shepherd's reputation-building process.[40] According to Campbell, a crucial moment in the development of a shepherd's reputation is his first quarrel. According to his observations, these fights, which usually take place in the local cafe, the village square, and other such public places, determine the shepherd's image and reputation.

This observation gives a broader interpretation to the findings of the University of Michigan experiment presented above. It basically explains why the crime patterns in the southern United States differ from those in the rest of the country. The South is characterized by more honor killings, but statistics show lower crime rates regarding other types of crime. In remote areas in the southern United States, the purpose of the violence is not economic gain. A man fights more for his honor.[41]

There is extensive literature on the reflection of culture in economic behaviors. One of the first to deal with this aspect was the sociologist, Max Weber,[42] who claimed that it is not economic forces that give rise to ideologies, but rather culture which gives rise to forms of economic behavior. For example, he argues that there is a connection between Protestantism (as a form of culture-based thinking) and economic behaviors. In Protestant countries, people's behavior is more closely linked to significant improvements in hygiene, savings, educational attainment, and per capita income.[43]

Studies examining the typical behaviors of communities and groups in contexts of economic behavior have clearly shown the relationship between culture as it has evolved in the historical process, and trust which is the important "glue" in collective economic behaviors. For example, Edward Banfield[44] studied social life in southern Italy after World War

II. He found that the degree of trust was extremely low and was, in fact, reserved only for the nuclear family. This fact has made it difficult to have enterprises that benefit the whole community (e.g., a public library). The culture of distrust on the one hand, and of only trusting the nuclear family on the other, originates in the history of the region that created phenomena like the Cosa Nostra.

From what has been presented, so far (the mere tip of the iceberg when discussing a complex subject such as *culture*) it is clear that: (a) Expressions of behavior derived from cultural differences can have greater variability than interpersonal differences; and (b) the cognitive patterns that result from culture have a historical background. That is, cultural components are shaped as an adaptive response to the environment and then *learned and passed down from generation to generation.*

The last point is interesting, and we have already encountered it in the mention of the comparative study between cultures of rice growers and wheat growers (Chapter 2). Studies, as well as the unmediated impressions of every person traveling in the world, clearly point to cross-cultural differences manifested in consistent and patterned behaviors. This can be seen in reference to time, work, authority, parent–child relationships, and more. In fact, almost every aspect of life is immersed, to one degree or another, in cultural patterns. Indeed, many studies deal with the description of intercultural differences as well as the everyday practical meanings of these differences.[45]

The interesting and somewhat astonishing question is: How is it that these norms – created hundreds and thousands of years ago around subsistence issues (e.g., rice and wheat growing) or herding, which created functional cultural practices for their time – continue to be passed down from generation to generation and remain "cultural compasses", long after they have seemingly lost their relevance? Furthermore, how can such "hereditary culture" be associated with patterns of choosing and following leaders in different groups?

The descendants of the cowboys in the southern United States have not herded cattle for generations. Descendants of rice growers in Japan and South Korea have not been engaged in this kind of work for many years (today, in developed countries, less than 3 percent of the population is able to provide for their agricultural consumption). Instead, they are engaged in the manufacture of cars and cell phones. The descendants of wheat growers no longer grow wheat, but work in high-tech, industrial production and various services. Yet, as comparative studies have shown, the individualism (as a cultural characteristic) of wheat growers and the collectivism of rice growers are still reflected in the daily practices of organizations. Toyota's corporate culture is much more collectivist, while Apple emphasizes personal development and achievement. There are countless anecdotes and studies describing the difficulty of intercultural encounters. Many companies that send representatives to a foreign country (re-location) make sure to provide their representatives with cultural training. It is clear today that for those without the ability to read the "cultural map" the ability to perform tasks can be impaired to the point of failure.

A multitude of evidence reflects the descriptive side of intercultural differences. It is also clear that culture is manifested in different sets of everyday norms and practices. What is less clear is: How are cultural norms and practices passed down from generation to generation? And most importantly: Why are seemingly outdated cultural norms and practices still being learned? The second question seems to contradict biological evolutionary logic, and raises speculations that cultural evolution may have its own logic. We will now discuss those aspects that also have implications regarding the issue of leadership and followership.

LEARNING AND ACQUIRING CULTURE-BASED NORMS AND PRACTICES

Learning takes place in nature in many and varied configurations. The simpler types of learning can be observed visually and the underlying mechanism can easily be deciphered. For example, field mice (*Peromyscus polionotus*) of a normal color are brown, and dig burrows in dark soil. But in the sand-colored dunes of Florida lives a species of the same biological origin, with very light-colored fur, known as the "beach mouse". The light color is an adaptation that disguises the mice from predators such as owls and herons. Such an adaptation is basically an existential learning mechanism in the face of threatening environmental conditions. This is, of course, evolutionary learning at its fundamental, biological level. The following case demonstrates a greater complexity of learning processes.

The giant Asian wasp is a predatory wasp that is especially common in Japan. It is the largest wasp in the world, about the length of a thumb. It is equipped with formidable jaws adapted to grasping and killing the insects it preys upon, and its stinger is half-an-inch long. With a wingspan of seven-and-a-half inches, it can fly at a rate of 40 miles per hour. Its maggots are fat, insatiable eating machines.

To satisfy their unstoppable demand for food, the adult wasps attack bee nests. The European honey bees brought to Asia are one of the main victims of the giant wasps. The onslaught on the honey bees' nest is manifested in a relentless massacre that has almost no parallel in nature. It begins when a lone wasp finds a nest. The wasp marks the doomed nest with a drop of pheromone, which it secretes from the tip of its belly near the entrance of the bee colony. Her friends in the nest, who are summoned by the pheromone signal, gather in a group of 20–30 wasps and prepare for battle against a colony of up to 30,000 honey bees.

But there is no real confrontation here. The wasps invade the hive, and with their murderous jaws, decapitate the bees one by one. Since each wasp can bite off a bee's head at a rate of 40 per minute, the battle ends within a few hours: All the bees die, the body parts pile up in the hive, and then the wasps fill their pantry. For a week, they systematically loot the nest, eating honey and carrying the helpless bee larvae to their nests, where they throw them into the open mouths of their offspring.

But some bees can fight back against the giant wasps: honey bees native to Japan. Their method of protection is fascinating and worth exploring. When the patrol wasp approaches the hive for the first time, the honey bees rush in and call their companions, while attempting to seduce the wasp and pull it into the hive. Meanwhile, hundreds of workers gather on the inside of the entrance. Once the wasp is inside the hive, it is covered in a tight ball comprised of masses of bees. By shaking their bellies, the bees raise the temperature inside the ball to 47 degrees Celsius. The bees can survive at such a temperature, but not the wasp. Within 20 minutes, the wasp boils to death and the nest is usually saved.

This example sheds light on more complex and sophisticated learning principles. First, the link between learning and environmental threat is immediately apparent. European honey bees grew up in a different environment that does not have giant carnivorous wasps, and so natural selection did not lead to the construction of defenses against them. Second, the learning of the Japanese honey bees is evident. This example shows a type of sophistication that goes beyond adaptive color change. Without this group cooperation of gathering and coordinating among the bees, the heat level necessary to kill the Asian wasp could not have been achieved. That is, the ability to collaborate and learn at the group level confers enormous adaptive benefits.

A systematic observation of animals and processes of the kind described at the beginning of the chapter emphatically points to the centrality of cooperation and learning. In most animals, learning is essential to the initial challenges of existence. Among humans, learning is much more complex, abstract, and distant from the pure biological contexts described in Chapter 1.

It is enough to observe, even superficially, the consistent behaviors of any group to recognize that their members exhibit behaviors that originate from culture; that is, behaviors that characterize members of a particular group which are absent in other groups. Moreover, they cannot be linked to the initial adaptation challenges described in the first chapter. For example, in a short time, secular children dress, speak, and behave differently from children their age who were born into ultra-Orthodox families living in the same geographical environment.

The source of these differences is *imitation learning*. The centrality as well as the mundaneness and the automatic mode of learning by imitation are exemplified in the following story told by the well-known evolutionary zoologist, Richard Dawkins, of Oxford University:

> As an undergraduate I was chatting to a friend in the Balliol College lunch queue. He regarded me with increasingly quizzical amusement, then asked: "Have you just been with Peter Brunet?" I had indeed, though I couldn't guess how he knew. Peter Brunet was our much loved tutor, and I had come hotfoot from a tutorial hour with him. "I thought so", my friend laughed. "You are talking just like him; your voice sounds exactly like his." I had, if only briefly, "inherited" intonations and manners of speech from an admired, and now greatly missed, teacher.
>
> Years later, when I became a tutor myself, I taught a young woman who affected an unusual habit. When asked a question which required deep thought, she would screw her eyes tight shut, jerk her head down to her chest and then freeze for up to half a minute before looking up, opening her eyes, and answering the question with fluency and intelligence. I was amused by this, and did an imitation of it to divert my colleagues after dinner. Among them was a distinguished Oxford philosopher. As soon as he saw my imitation, he immediately said: "That's Wittgenstein! Is her surname … by any chance?" Taken aback, I said that it was. "I thought so", said my colleague. "Both her parents are professional philosophers and devoted followers of Wittgenstein." The gesture had passed from the great philosopher, via one or both of her parents to my pupil. I suppose that, although my further imitation was done in jest, I must count myself a fourth-generation transmitter of the gesture. And who knows where Wittgenstein got it?[46]

An area of research called "natural pedagogy"[47] focuses on imitation learning in infancy. Its importance for our discussion lies in the fact that studies in this area point to the most initial and natural way of human learning in a context that is relevant to learning cultural norms and practices. As such, these studies provide us with insights that will help us to expand our discussion of the cultural context of leadership.

The following experiment by Professor Andrew Meltzoff,[48] a developmental psychologist at the University of Washington in the United States, demonstrates findings and a way of thinking that characterizes natural pedagogy research. In the experiment, infants sat on their mother's lap in front of an experimenter (a "large figure" in infants' eyes). The experimenter looked into the baby's eyes, looked at a "magic box" that was lying on her desk and then did a surprising thing: she leaned forward with her head toward the box and lit a light bulb placed on top of the box by pressing it with her forehead. A week later, the babies were returned to the lab and were allowed to play in front of the box. What did the babies do then? Most of the babies spontaneously leaned toward the box and turned on the light bulb using their foreheads. They *accurately mimicked* the experimenter's behavior.

Other similarly conducted experiments without expression of intentional personal reference to the infant (eye contact is the most prominent feature of such a reference) showed that the infant's faithful imitation (lighting the bulb with the forehead) was far less frequent and that infants tended to light the bulb in the most efficient manner compared to other forms of learning. This experiment points to the strongest and fastest form of learning (e.g., trial and error): learning to imitate from a demonstration model (a large figure). The experiment's strong effect (14-month-old babies who light a bulb with their forehead, after only one demonstration, and a week-long time-lapse) is conditioned by a kind of unique communication "syntax": a personal and directed approach to the baby and then a demonstration conducted for him/her. The communicative function of this "syntax" is to signal to the infant that the new adaptive message invested in him by the "large figure" (in such an exclusive way) is specifically aimed at him for his personal use.[49]

Similar experiments in the domain of epistemic trust (trust people grant to knowledge transferred from authority figures) indicate that in adaptive situations of new learning in an uncertain environment, humans – from the beginning of their development and throughout their adulthood – tend to place great trust in a figure perceived as competent (markers of expertise, prestige, and status) and generous (markers of intentional communication, belonging, and precious demonstration).[50]

The result of this learning is a kind of behavioral "anomaly": a rapid transition below the threshold of awareness from behavior based on practical rationality: emulation – what is effective (in the case of the described experiment – lighting the bulb with one's hands), to another system, unique to humans, collective and normative in its essence: faithful imitation of what is "right" (lighting the bulb with one's forehead), but not necessarily efficient.[51]

To precede the latter a little, this transition between the two human motivational systems – from the cost–benefit-oriented system to the normative system – is a salient feature of the influence we call "charismatic", and is intrinsically related to the unique ability of humans to use agents to pass on collective knowledge, norms, and practices from generation to generation in a rapid and extremely efficient manner (without the need for trial and error) and thus accumulate cultural capital.[52]

Let us now return to the discussion on cultural differences. In fact, Meltzoff's experiment and others like it point to a *universal pattern* of learning that illuminates the foundations of the formation of intercultural differences. As in the experiment, but in a way that is mundane and systematic, children are exposed to their parents and other authority figures and imitate them, oftentimes unconsciously.

When the conditions described in the experiment are met in daily life – that is, a personal reference, and constant demonstration – the imitation is fast, accurate, and very determined. Thus, children who at the beginning of their lives may exhibit very similar behavior and reactions anywhere in the world will slowly grow up and become quite different regarding their language, clothing, and symbols. In addition, the informative signals that cause them to feel excitement, anger, and other emotions will also differ.

As mentioned, the ultra-Orthodox male child will tend to dress like his father, imitate his father's movements in the synagogue, and develop certain aspirations and expectations related to the models to which he has been exposed. He will differ from a child his age who has been exposed to and imitated other types of large figures. Thus, through a universal learning process different cultural groups are created.

A dramatic demonstration of this emerged in recordings heard in an investigation conducted after a Korean air plane crash in Guam.[53] Landing in Guam is considered relatively simple. Guam Airport has a so-called "Glide Slope", a kind of giant radio signal spotlight that rises from the airport into the sky, and the pilot simply follows the radio beam on the way to the runway. On the night of the accident, the beam of light was not activated because the equipment had been sent for repairs. The pilots were notified in advance. It wasn't considered a big deal and wasn't supposed to cause any difficulties. However, unfortunately, the weather conditions were more problematic than usual, due to large amounts of rain.

In the transcription of the conversations that took place in the cockpit, the typical respectful attitude toward authority which characterizes Korean culture was expressed – this time with fatal results. The first officer was heard saying to the captain in dismay: "Don't you think the rain is heavy?" (In the language of a culture devoid of such levels of respect to authority, the translation would be something like: "The weather is absolutely awful. It's dark outside, the floodlight is off, and we have no backup plan").

However, in Korean culture you can't speak in this manner. So, the first officer hinted. In his opinion, he'd said everything he could say to his senior officer. The (flight) engineer answered, "Radar weather is helping us." This, too, is something of an understatement, and sounds puzzling to Western ears. He was actually telling the captain: "On a night like this, you can't rely on your eyes to land the plane. You have to look carefully at what the weather radar is telling us." However, within this Korean team, the communication differed from that of similar teams from most Western countries – where the *speaker* has a responsibility to convey messages clearly and if there is a danger, to do so more vigorously, and even firmly. In Korea, as in other cultures characterized by respect and reverence for authority, the *listener* (rather than the speaker) is responsible for clarifying what's been said.

According to the interpretation given in the research, the cultural component apparently played a significant role in the Guam crash. This can be said with a degree of confidence because this is in no way an exceptional example.[54]

Research in natural pedagogy is of great importance in this context because it illuminates the "beginning of the axes" of cultural learning, and its transmission at the intergenerational level through the process of imitation. In fact, these studies can be seen as a convergence of the initial learning of cultural norms.

These studies not only sharpen the way in which the degree of imitation is created. They also point to what happens in the most basic initial connection between a small figure and a large figure. Beyond the asymmetrical structure, there is, as described, a very specific communication process: a personal address (e.g., eye contact), which creates a feeling that the small figure is the exclusive recipient of the reference. Then, there is the reference itself, and following it, the demonstration of an action or behavior. There is a pattern of communication that strengthens trust in the large figure.

Thus, we would seem to have a pattern that is indeed being studied and presented as a form of natural pedagogy that can be experimentally researched, but, in fact, it is a pattern that indicates conditions for creating *trust and influence* in their initial pre-verbal, "pure" configuration. There is an insight here which is relevant to leadership and followership. This trust is activated when the recipient feels that the "strong and wise" is also generous, that is, signals to him/her that s/he is offering adaptive knowledge that is particularly relevant to him/her. We now have a research framework that can help us understand the foundations of the influence created between individuals and large figures, in general, and leaders as a distinct case of this category.

This is an important explanation. However, it is not comprehensive enough to clarify why a person who is clearly a leader in one group will not necessarily be a leader in another group. Why can certain individuals be the undisputed leader of one group that has distinct cultural characteristics, but have no influence at all over other groups that have other cultural characteristics? To understand this, we must return to the evolutionary cause of different cultures and the relevant mechanisms for deciphering the foundations of influence of large figures in specific cultural contexts.

The crucial difference between human cognition and that of other species is in the ability to cooperate with others in relation to common and complex goals.[55] This ability for "shared attention" is the initial basis of the phenomenon that is so familiar to us: that of social categorization – the very human characteristic of "we" versus "they", which is so deeply ingrained in our social lives.[56]

Throughout the cultural evolution of human beings, with the expansion of the small group and the development of competition among groups, each group has had to frame itself, build unique practices in the struggle for survival against other groups, and act in coordination and with cooperation.

With the growth of the small group from family and small tribe to peoples and nations, it was also necessary to move from tangible group assets (tools of war or cooking, unique methods, etc.) to increasingly abstract assets that can connect and coordinate members of a large group where not everyone knows everyone else. Thus, the language was perfected and group symbols, norms, and stable traditions were constructed to enable functioning beyond the here-and-now dynamics. The result was a unique model of life that required a different cognitive and motivational adaptation: the cognitive ability for abstract representation and the motivation for inward loyalty (we), and outward aggression (they). Indeed, humans have a unique ability in the animal kingdom to identify, diagnose, and interpret both informative and symbolic informative signals.[57]

We mentioned this briefly in the opening chapter. Animals recognize a small range of manifestations, especially those related to soma or reproduction – behaviors related to fear (body contraction) or aggression (e.g., standing which indicates a readiness to pounce), expressions of sexuality, and so on. Humans have an impressive ability to recognize intentions without occurrence that has a distinct behavioral expression.[58]

A woman sitting in a cafe is able to discern from a glance that the man sitting at a nearby table likes her. A child can see from the expression on his mother's face that she is angry with him. People can watch TV and infer that an interviewee resents a question, even if he does not raise his voice. People can also feel when there is or isn't "chemistry" between others who happen to be in their company – even if nothing happens or nothing is said. In short, looks, facial expressions, certain body movements, forms of dress, and so on are all hints from which a person can understand various intentions and a great deal of information. This social skill is, of course, an important catalyst for the ability to cooperate, which is particularly distinct among human beings. Humans, better than any other creature, can cook a complex dinner with others with almost no talking, write an article or book with others, or develop a start-up idea in a group.

Another advantage of the human race lies in its impressive ability to learn. As we have seen in natural pedagogy studies, imitation learning takes place as early as infancy. However, learning exists and appears in different and varied ways and becomes especially significant in group configurations. For example, people do not just learn from their own personal experience. They also learn from observing others (vicarious learning). Life in groups, starting with the family, sports team, a youth movement group, a military group, or a task group at work allows for very quick exposure to the deliberations, successes, and failures of others and hence learning "what works" and what does not work in this group. These are learning processes that have been discussed and researched extensively, and have an impact on the functioning of both the individual and the group.[59]

In fact, much of the research on organizations attests to this. The main reason for the existence of organizations is the fact that organizations can do and learn what the individual cannot perform alone. Organizations are most often clusters built to perform tasks. This observation of "task grouping" processes immediately puts the spotlight on the centrality of *coordination processes*.

Indeed, as Henry Mintzberg[60] has shown in his work on organizations, understanding the coordination mechanisms in organizations is key to understanding how they function. For example, in organizations where production is standard (e.g., mass production industries such as textiles, food, or car manufacturing), the final production unit is divided into hundreds or thousands of small task units made by humans or robots that repeat the same "task unit" (e.g., threading – as portrayed in Chaplin's movie *Modern Times*). *Standardization* is a principle that regulates the coordination of hundreds and thousands of tasks that are grouped into the final output unit (e.g., jeans, automobile production). Most tasks are not carried out at that standardization level. They require assessment of the situation, judgment, and especially coordination between different abilities and specializations. The head of a research and development team in a high-tech industry that includes physicists, programmers, information systems experts, and mathematicians is, first and foremost, a function of the coordination and integration of the team. Without this cooperation, there will usually be no progress and the chances of chaotic conduct are high. In other words, without a leader, the pooling of group resources, the ability to coordinate group work, including its ability to learn and improve, will not come to fruition.

This is a main principle that explains the centrality of leadership at the forefront of evolutionary development. In this respect, the hunter-gatherer period (as far as we can understand their lives by observing groups that have preserved this way of life, such as the Hadza tribe in northern Tanzania) can attest that the smaller of such groups learned to work as a team without a prominent need for a leader. But moving away from the way of life of an organic team whose coordination was largely built-in to the very close bond among team members created a need to develop mechanisms whose purpose is coordination. The activity simply became too complex. The leader, as noted, was mainly a coordination mechanism, through which distinct group advantages were created in the existential struggle.[61] This is perhaps one of the reasons we have evidence of leaders in later periods. In terms of the development of human history, the question of leadership apparently became more central as human societies began to be characterized by farming, fishing, and herding.

The development of symbolic abilities expanded the range of possibilities of the leader's influence beyond the basic function of task coordination. As noted, groups began to develop a variance that was expressed in different symbols. The various symbols intensified distinct group identities, thus expanding the leader's coordination function to become, in many cases, one of the symbols of group identity (which sometimes became one of the sources of its power in the struggle with other groups). From this perspective, the leader, as the French sociologist Emile Durkheim[62] argued, is the embodiment of the group, he is a kind of "ideal member of the group" – the figure that the members of the group want to imitate.

A clear example of this argument is a well-known group of Orthodox religious Jews known as the "Chabad group", scattered all over the world. They preserve their group identity through their mythological leader – the Rebbe of Lubavitch. Although he has been dead for many years, the group members continue not only to glorify him, but to convey messages that are supposedly his and on his behalf. This serves to reinforce the argument about the symbolic role of the leader as the "glue of the group". Through the mechanism of telling stories about him, members of the Chabad group create and preserve distinct cultural norms and practices that enhance group identity.

In an interpretation that is consistent with the evolutionary paradigm, group identity can confer benefits. A strong group identity can promote a greater degree of cooperation. It is easier for group members who speak the same language and have a world of similar symbolic associations to communicate within themselves than to communicate with others who are not partners in their symbolic world.[63]

The arguments in the chapter relevant to understanding the influence of authority figures (including leaders) on people can be summarized as follows: (a) There is a universal pattern of influence on people. This pattern consists of a small figure and a large figure and a very specific communication pattern maintained by the large figure. The communication pattern that creates maximum influence includes: personal reference, reference to an object, and demonstration (action, behavior, statement). This dynamic can be seen in its expression from infancy, but further down the road this pattern is also noticeable. (b) During evolution, the group became a key component in human development and the leader became one of the important catalysts in the group's existence and function.

Along these lines, the attraction to leaders as protective, teaching, unifying, and coordinating symbols is universal, and exists in all groups.

However, each and every group leadership mediates its unique content (which we call *culture*).

An analysis of famous speeches given by leaders clearly points to the emotional aspects inherent in the "natural pedagogy" component, and in the emphasis on group identity.[64] When listening to speeches, words, and sentences in which there is a noticeable awakening of applause, one can clearly identify these elements. The loudest applause was given to Martin Luther King in his famous "I Have a Dream" speech, when he first addressed the notion of group identity and distinguished it with the demand and hope that this group would be like other "privileged" groups. These arguments became especially exciting when they contained a personal expression, such as MLK expressing the wish that one day his children would be able to join hands with white children. Indeed, one can easily find the personal reference component, the reference to a personal vision and the use of group symbols in most of the speeches that have entered the pantheon of "great speeches".[65]

Now that we have a conceptual framework which can be used to analyze both the universal component and the local-cultural component of leadership, we will use this framework to analyze some familiar leadership manifestations. The best-known ones are those considered to be "charismatic" across the board.

NOTES

1. Kets de Vries, Manfred (1988). Prisoners of leadership. *Human Relations*, 41(31), 261–80.
2. De Dreu, Caresten K. and Kret, Mariska E. (2015). Oxytocin conditions intergroup relations through unregulated in-group empathy, cooperation, conformity and defense. *Biological Psychiatry*, 79(3), 165–73.
3. Bowlby, John (1969). *Attachment and Loss, Vol. 1: Attachment*. New York: Basic Books. Bowlby, John (1973). *Attachment and Loss, Vol. 2: Separation*. New York: Basic Books. Bowlby, John (1980). *Attachment and Loss, Vol. 3: Loss, Sadness and Depression*. New York: Basic Books.
4. Erikson, Eric H. (1969). *Gandhi's Truth: On the Origins of Militant Non-Violence*. New York: Norton.
5. Cassidy, Jude and Shaver, Philip (eds) (2018). *Handbook of Attachment. Theory, Research and Clinical Applications*, 3rd edn. New York: Guilford Publications.
6. Hazan, Cindy and Shaver, Philip (1987). Romantic love conceptualized as an attachment process. *Journal of Personality and Social Psychology*, 52, 511–24.

7. Mayseless, Ofra, Sharabany, Ruth, and Sagi, Avi (1997). Attachment concerns of others as manifested in parental, spousal and friendship relationships. *Personal Relationships*, 4, 255–69.
8. Shalit, Alon, Popper, Micha, and Zakay, Dan (2010). Followers' attachment styles and their preference for social or personal charismatic leaders. *Leadership and Organizational Development Journal*, 31(5), 458–72.
9. Mayseless, Ofra and Popper, Micha (2019). Attachment and leadership: Review and new insights. *Current Opinion in Psychology*, February 25, 157–71.
10. Hill, Melvin. A. (1984). The law of the father: Leadership and symbolic authority in psychoanalysis. In B. Kellerman (ed.), *Leadership: Multidisciplinary Perspectives*. Englewood Cliffs, NJ: Prentice Hall, pp. 128–40.
11. Schlesinger, Arthur M. Jr. (1958). *The Coming of the New Deal*. Boston: Houghton Mifflin, pp. 1–2.
12. Hertzler, J.O. (1940). Crises and dictatorships. *American Sociological Review*, 5, 157–69.
13. Boehm, Christopher (1999). *Hierarchy in the Forest*. London: Harvard University Press.
14. Todorov, Alexander, Mandisodza, Ansu, Goren, Amir, and Hall, Crysta C. (2005). Inferences of competence from faces predict election outcomes. *Science*, 308 (June), 1623–6.
15. Olivola, Christopher Y. and Todorov, Alexander (2010). Elected in 100 milliseconds: Appearance-based trait. Inference and voting. *Journal of Nonverbal Behavior*, 34, 83–110.
16. Antonakis, John and Dalgas, Olaf (2009). Predicting elections: Child's play. *Science*, 232, February, 1183.
17. Gladwell, Malcolm (2005). *Blink. The Power of Thinking without Thinking*. London: Penguin Books.
18. Popper, Micha (2012). *Fact and Fantasy about Leadership*. Cheltenham, UK and Northampton, MA, USA: Edward Elgar.
19. Kosinski, Jersey (1972). *Being There*. New York: Bantam Books.
20. Conger, Jay A. and Kanungo, Rabindra N. (1987). Toward a behavioral theory of charismatic leadership in organizational settings. *Academy of Management Review*, 12, 637–47.
21. Popper, *Fact and Fantasy about Leadership*, p. 35.
22. Ibid.
23. Asch, Solomon (1946). Framing impressions of personality. *Journal of Abnormal and Social Psychology*, 41, 258–90.
24. Woodward, Bob (2018). *Fear: Trump in the White House*. New York: Simon & Schuster.
25. Boehm, *Hierarchy in the Forest*.
26. Fiske, Susan T., Cuddy, Amy J.C., and Glick, Peter (2007). Universal dimensions of social cognition: Warmth and competence. *Trends in Cognitive Sciences*, 11(2), 77–83.
27. Gladwell, *Blink*.

28. Popper, Micha (2013). Leaders perceived as distant or close: Some implications for psychological theory on leadership. *Leadership Quarterly*, 24, 1–8.
29. Bass, Bernard M. (2008). *The Bass Handbook of Leadership*, 4th edn. New York: Free Press.
30. Avolio, Bruce, Bass, Bernard M., and Jung Dong I. (1999). Re-examining the components of transformational and transactional leadership using the Multifactor Leadership Questionnaire. *Journal of Occupational and Organizational Psychology*, 72, 441–62.
31. Laurence, Janice H. and Mathews, Michael D. (2012). *The Oxford Handbook of Military Psychology*. New York: Oxford University Press.
32. Gabriel, Richard A. and Savage, Paul L. (1978). *Crisis in Command*. New York: Hill and Wang.
33. Gardner, William, Cogliser, C.C., Davis, Kelly M., and Dickens, Matthew P. (2011). Authentic leadership: A review of the literature and research agenda. *Leadership Quarterly*, 22, 1120–45.
34. Goldhagen, Daniel Jonah (1996). *Ordinary Germans and the Holocaust*. New York: Alfred A. Knopf.
35. Ibid., p. 242.
36. Elon, Amos (2004). *Pity It All: A Portrait of Jews in Germany, 1743–1933*. New York: Penguin Books.
37. Klein, Katherine and House, Robert (1995). On fire: Charismatic leadership and level of analysis. *Leadership Quarterly*, 6(2), 183–98.
38. Gladwell, Malcolm (2008). *Outliers*. New York. Little Brown and Company, p. 154.
39. Nisbett, Richard E. and Cohen, Dov (1996). *Culture of Honor: The Psychology of Violence in the South*. Boulder, CO: Westview Press.
40. Campbell, John K. (1970). Honor and the devil. In J.G. Peristiany (ed.), *Honor and Shame: The Values of Mediterranean Society*. Chicago, IL: University of Chicago Press, pp. 141–70.
41. Reed, J.S. (1982). *One South: An Ethnic Approach to Regional Culture*. Baton Rouge, LA: Louisiana State University Press.
42. Weber, Max (1968). *Economy and Society*. New York: Bedminster Press.
43. Tawney, Richard H. (1962). *Religion and the Rise of Capitalism*. New York: Harcourt Brace.
44. Banfield, Edward (1958). *The Moral Basis of Backward Society*. Glencoe, IL: Free Press.
45. Hofstede, Geert (1997). *Cultures and Organizations: The Software of the Mind*. New York: McGraw-Hill.
46. Dawkins, Richard (1999). Introduction to Susan Blackmore's book: *The Meme Machine*. Oxford: Oxford University Press, p. 1.
47. Csibra, Gergely and Gergely, Gyorgy (2011). Natural pedagogy as evolutionary adaptation. *Philosophical Transactions of the Royal Society of London B: Biological Sciences*, 366(1567), 1149–57.
48. Meltzoff, Andrew. N. (1988). Infant imitation after a 1-week delay: Long-term memory for novel acts and multiple stimuli. *Developmental Psychology*, 24(4), 470.

49. Gardiner, A.K., Greif, M.L., and Bjork Lund, D.F. (2011). Guided by intention: Preschoolers' imitation reflects inferences of causation. *Journal of Cognition and Development*, 12(3), 355–73.
50. Buttelmann, D., Zmyj, N., Daum, M., and Carpenter, M. (2013). Selective imitation of in-group over out-group members in 14-month-old infants. *Child Development*, 84(2), 422–8. Henrich, J. (2009). The evolution of costly displays, cooperation and religion: Credibility enhancing displays and their implications for cultural evolution. *Evolution and Human Behavior*, 30(4), 244–60.
51. Boyd, R., Richerson, P.J., and Henrich, J. (2011). The cultural niche: Why social learning is essential for human adaptation. *Proceedings of the National Academy of Sciences USA*, 108(Suppl. 2), 10918–25.
52. Gergely, Gyorgey and Jacob, Pierr (2012). Reasoning about instrumental and communicative agency in human infancy. *Advances in Child Development and Behavior*, 43, 59–94.
53. Gladwell, *Outliers*, p. 177.
54. Ibid.
55. Tomasello, Michael and Rakoczy, Hanes (2003). What makes human cognition unique? From individual to shared collective intentionality. *Mind and Language*, 18, 121–47.
56. Tomasello, Michael (2014). *A Natural History of Human Thinking*. Cambridge, MA: Harvard University Press.
57. Ibid.
58. Ibid.
59. Boyd, Robert and Richerson, Peter J. (2005). *The Origin and Evolution of Cultures*. Oxford: Oxford University Press.
60. Mintzberg, Henry (1979). *The Structuring of Organizations: A Synthesis of the Research*. Englewood Cliffs, NJ: Prentice Hall.
61. Van Vugt, Mark, Hogan, Robert, and Kaiser, Robert B. (2008). Leadership, followership, and evolution. *American Psychologist*, 63(3), 182–96.
62. Durkheim, Emile (1973). The dualism of human nature and its social conditions. In R. Bellah (ed.), *Emile Durkheim on Morality and Society*. Chicago, IL: University of Chicago Press.
63. Popper, Micha and Castelnovo, Omri (2018). The function of great leaders in human culture: A cultural-evolutionary perspective. *Leadership*, 14(6), 757–74.
64. Shamir, Boas, Michael B. Arthur, and Robert J. House (1994). The rhetoric of charismatic leadership: A theoretical extension, a case study and implications for research. *Leadership Quarterly*, 5(1), 25.
65. Brosh, Tamar (1993). *Neum lechol att (Speech at all times)*. Tel Aviv: Yediot Sefarim Publishing (Hebrew).

4. Charisma

Charisma is a type of phenomenon that is mostly "felt".[1] Indeed, observing audiences that respond to the speeches of figures such as Martin Luther King or Muhammad Ali exemplifies the expression of emotions to the point of ecstatic manifestations. That is, one can observe distinct public reactions to charismatic figures compared to figures who are not experienced as such. The charismatic figure evokes stronger emotions. We will first try to pinpoint the fundamental characteristics of any charisma-related phenomenon.

The most common characteristic to all charismatics – whether an actor, a university lecturer, or a leader – is the distinct attention they attract. This is a cornerstone in understanding processes of influence. It is not for nothing that phrases like "magnetic effect" or "hypnotic effect" are used when talking about a person who is conspicuously attractive. Indeed, in interviews conducted with followers of prominent charismatic leaders, the attraction to the leader is described in terms of hypnosis. In extreme cases, followers have been attentive to their leaders to the point of exhaustion, drink their words in thirstily, and in some cases merge their own identity with that of the leader.

In the most extreme cases, the followers were willing to do anything the leader asked. Particularly appalling evidence of this is the case of the largest mass suicide in modern history, which occurred in 1978, when the cult leader, Reverend Jim Jones, ordered his followers to commit suicide. All 911 of his believers did so, out of a sense of deep conviction. The proof of the extent of Jones's influence was not only in the willingness of his believers to commit suicide, but in their willingness to also kill their children (about 200 children died in the mass suicide).[2]

There are early attempts to understand the origins and patterns of this "magnetic phenomenon". Anton Franz Mesmer (1734–1815), considered the father of modern medical hypnosis, was the first to investigate this issue. He developed the theory of "animal magnetism", later referred to as "Mesmerism". This theory propounded that the human body contains an invisible fluid with magnetic properties that is influenced by the body's harmony with nature and affects our behavior.[3]

Along the way, and in light of his therapeutic experience, Mesmer came to the conclusion that his very connection with his patients and the processes they were undergoing was influential. Indeed, the hypnotic process he describes includes the same elements that constitute cornerstones of influence at the group level: emphasizing the group's uniqueness, isolation from the world, leading a group trance through certain gestures (including symbolic aspects such as dress, music, etc.). In short: building conditions of attention to the "magician", who provides the group members with unifying emotional signals.

Liberation from everything, while merging with a group entity embodied in the leader, was well expressed by those people who, for various reasons, "missed" the mass suicide committed under the inspiration of Jim Jones. One of them, for example, who happened to be at the scene of the suicide after it happened, cried bitterly. When they tried to comfort him, he said: "I wanted to die with my friends, I wanted to die with Jim, I wanted to do what they did ... ."[4]

This case demonstrates attention and persuasion processes at their most extreme level – the hypnotic level. However, attention that carries a significant impact is also created in everyday life contexts, which are not necessarily dramatic or outstanding in any way. For example, one can see a distinct demonstration of attention in a grandfather's ability to tell his grandson a story, in a way that distracts him from all other stimuli and grabs all of his attention.

A large group's attention may become riveted when listening to a fascinating story told at a storytelling festival. Such attention can intensify if the person who is the object of attention is famous – an artist, a famous writer, a leader. Shared attention means that many minds are synchronized in a similar process, as if at a certain point in time, many minds meld to become one collective mind.

Indeed, this idea was studied under laboratory conditions at the neurological level by a group of researchers from Princeton University.[5] Subjects in the lab listened to a "good" story under the scrutiny of an FMRI scanner. Before the story began, the listeners' brain activity patterns were measured and shown to be varied, but once the story began, something unusual happened. The responses in the social areas of the brain synchronized and became very similar – a phenomenon defined by the researchers as *neural entrainment*.

This synchronizing effect depends on the meaning of the story to the listeners, and is amplified as long as there is a common denominator of values, knowledge, and beliefs shared by the group exposed to the object of attention. For example, a group of ultra-Orthodox Jews will listen attentively (and in great synchronicity) to the weekly sermon of their revered Rabbi, while for a secular group the same sermon will be an incomprehensible speech that does not attract their attention.

Studies show that the sense of belonging to a group is deeply entrenched in the individual, and helps him/her to synchronize with other group members even when they are alone.[6]

The origins of these synchronizing abilities are evolutionary. Researchers studying infant developmental processes have pointed this out in experiments.[7] Infants are immediately sensitive at the beginning of their lives to very specific signals such as eye contact, smiling, and empathetic tones – signals to which the responses indicate the existence of certain inherent sensitivities, the purpose of which is to establish an attention span that is necessary for collaboration that promotes learning and adaptation.[8]

The findings of these studies are consistent with John Bowlby's attachment theory, which propounds that the inherent longing for a stronger and wiser figure is anchored, as noted, in existential evolutionary need. This process begins after birth and increases over time, through symbolic means. It is a kind of wireless connection that takes place through signals between the large figure and the small (needy) figure, which in certain circumstances generates high-level brain synchronization. However, this is not only about the dynamics of signals that exist between a small and a large figure, but also about group processes.

Humans have a grouping ability that does not necessarily exist on a genetic basis.[9] Humans have the ability to recognize symbols, social cues, gestures of affection, and common interests – all of which have measurable expressions.[10] An obvious conclusion is that common attention can be formed between a group and a large figure when circumstances cause the individuals' brains to become synchronized, as a collective entity. In this case, they all form a sort of single brain that responds collectively to certain signals.

According to this argument, charisma is first and foremost a phenomenon which originates in *shared attention*. It is built on the innate ability of human beings to synchronize their emotions, thoughts, and behaviors with one another, until they function as one coordinated and efficient body with a high level of continuous adaptive ability.

The origins of human synchronization abilities are physiological. It starts with coordination between the mother and the baby (while the baby is still in the womb), but its continuation is related to humans' highly developed ability to be "moved" by symbols through the institutionalization of shared attention. Shared attention may be caused by intentional personal communication, referral to an event or state of affairs, and demonstration, and a large figure can also emerge as a collective symbol, even if he is not instrumental at a particular moment (as in Meltzoff's experiment in which the infants lit the bulb with their forehead).

The unique power of the discussed communication acts is in changing human beings' learning and motivational pattern – from one that is essentially personal and immediate cost–benefit oriented to a normative and collective which is beyond the instrumental logic of the affected person ("from me, you will see and do"), and whose purpose is not a clear and immediate gain for the individual, but is rather beneficial to the group. This is a universal influence process that serves all cultures.

Based on early infrastructures of group belonging and shared cultural symbols, a leader can create a strong and unique influence for one group (with less meaning, if any, for another group). Hence, we point out that evolutionarily, charisma can be a catalyst for human ability – both biologically and symbolically-culturally – to turn individuals into a coordinated group force that develops and zealously preserves its existence.

Charisma, as noted earlier, is not necessarily related to objective dimensions (such as height). A person who is 2 meters tall, will be considered a tall person in any group. However, a person who is charismatic in one group will not necessarily be perceived as such in another group. Moreover, a person perceived as charismatic in the eyes of a particular public may, as described in the opening chapter, later lose his/her charisma in the eyes of that very public. Take, for example, Churchill, the iconic leader, who was not elected prime minister at the end of World War II. This is because his charismatic and inspiring leadership during the war was seen as irrelevant to the restoration of the British economy.

There are also examples of leaders who at one time were unappreciated, controversial, and even largely hated, who later became icons of charisma. One such case is that of Abraham Lincoln, who is considered the most revered president in US history. More streets, cities, and towns in the United States bear his name compared to other former presidents. His name has won the most mentions in the leading press and in the Library of Congress. Many cars, banknotes, and monuments also bear Lincoln's name. The interesting point in this case is that admiration for Lincoln as a charismatic leader only began to appear in the twentieth century, decades after he had already been all but forgotten (he was assassinated in 1865). This admiration reached its peak in 1922 – with the erection of the Lincoln Memorial in the US capital, Washington, DC.[11]

These examples sharpen the argument that if one wants to decipher the regularity of the phenomenon of leaders' charisma, the key to this is understanding the formation of followers' emotions toward leaders. This principle was understood as noted by the well-known German sociologist, Max Weber, who put this observation "on the map".[12] From this point of view, the conceptual framework discussed so far provides us with the necessary concepts and tools for analyzing the origins of charisma.

The universal aspect in the pattern discussed above clarifies two components that are inherent in people's attraction to leaders: neediness and greatness. This combination occurs naturally at the beginning of life – children (small figures) need adults (large figures). This is, as we have seen, the basic pattern in natural pedagogy studies, which is, in fact, the most basic pattern for understanding the formation of charisma. We will examine this argument through several instances of prominent charismatic leadership.

NEEDINESS AND GREATNESS

Neediness, as mentioned, is a salient characteristic of the "small figure". In infants, this characterization is objective. The baby, as described in theories like those of John Bowlby, needs a large figure simply to survive. However, the experience of needing a "large figure" is not exclusive to infants. This need can be intensively experienced by adults as well. This is how people feel when nature hits them with earthquakes or deadly storms. This is how the exhausted, hungry and frightened warrior feels during battle – when he fervently hopes his commander will "rescue" him; this is how fired workers feel when their workplace closes down. And this is how most of us feel in situations of uncertainty and lack of control.

Indeed, most reports and analyses of the emergence and rise of charismatic leaders involve a link to situations of crisis and uncertainty.[13] At such times, a sense of need is created in its purest expression. There is a kind of emotional retreat back to the basic pattern described above. In these situations, the charismatic leader is the "large figure". The combination of "neediness and seeking greatness" allows for a more focused look at the universal fundamental elements of charisma.

Hitler's rise is perhaps the most dramatic and documented example in history – not only of illustrating charisma as a result of a connection between being in need and greatness, but also in that it is a rare opportunity to carry out an in-depth examination of followers' need to create a "large figure" for themselves. A thorough examination of the events and processes clearly shows the discussed link as it appeared during two separate periods. The first period was a "trailer" for the great show that took place in the 1930s with Hitler's election as Chancellor.

This trailer sheds light on the psychological principles regarding the *universal* antecedents of charisma. Hitler's charisma began to emerge in 1923, which was a year of terrible crisis. Beyond the French invasion of the Ruhr region, the German coffers were depleted, German currency was worthless, and inflation became a dizzying vortex. The value of German currency dropped from 20 marks to the dollar on the eve of World War I to 972 marks in January 1923, and the mark dropped further later. In mid-September, the price of a kilogram of butter was 168 million marks. Whole life savings were wiped out within hours. Insurance policies were not worth the paper they were written on. Recipients of income and pensions saw everything disappear before their eyes. By then, the Nazi movement, which numbered a total of 55,000 members, already understood that Hitler's rhetorical ability was a driving force. Indeed, they were on the verge of seizing power in Bavaria, which, as is well known, failed and led Hitler to prison.

Hitler's charisma lost its fertilizers. Despite the effective use of the prison period to write *Mein Kampf,* and the attempts to glorify his image, the improved economic situation "reduced" Hitler's charisma. Almost like an experiment in social psychology, Hitler's charisma began to blossom again with the outbreak of the great economic crisis in the United States in 1929 and the seepage of its effect into Germany in the early 1930s. This periodic division sheds light on the link between neediness and seeking greatness in two senses: (a) as regards the complex meaning of a sense of being in need – on the part of the followers – and (b) regarding the psycho-sociological processes underlying the creation of "greatness". These two components are intertwined, and together form an integral part of the process of building charisma.

It seems that the universal principles underlying the interaction between a "small figure", who needs a "large figure" who is experienced and perceived as "knowing, protecting, caring and being a problem solver", are indeed clearest and purest when it comes to observations and experiments with infants. However, it seems that in crisis situations that take place in the lives of older people, it is possible, although more complex, to see these same principles in action.

The aforementioned metaphor of "charisma as fire" – which takes place within the spark-lighter-(leader)-"sensitive" combustibles (followers) oxygen that feeds the fire (accelerating circumstances) framework – can shed light on the analysis of the phenomenon. We will begin this discussion with the nature of the "combustibles": that is, does the cultural component instilled in infancy make some publics more "flammable" – more prone than others to charismatic influences? Are there cultural differences between various collectives on this question?

Such a discussion touches, in one way or another, on the issue of the roots of nationalism. Unlike many social scientists who see modernity, equal civil rights, language, and territory as the basis for nationalities and nation states,[14] other scholars believe that the roots of nationalism lie in the primary human feelings of belonging, solidarity, and cooperation among remnants of common culture.[15] That is, national sentiments have evolutionary roots. These affinities, which extend from the family to the tribe and ethnos, became central in politics with the emergence of states, many years before the "modern invention" of the nation state. Ethnicity has always been political, as people have always tended to favor those who were considered a part of their community and culture. Indeed, ethnic and national identities are among the most resilient and powerful of cultural identities. Ethnic and national affiliations have deep roots in the human psyche and have always been among the most powerful forces in human history.

Historical examples illustrating this argument are not lacking: Why did French Indochina disintegrate into separate nation states with decolonization instead of remaining a single unit like Dutch Indonesia? This is because countries from the modern Indochinese Peninsula have a long history and a nationally identified ethnic core that makes up about 85 percent of their population. These include: a Vietnamese country since the tenth century; the Cambodian-Khmer state since the sixth century; the Siamese-Thai state since the fourteenth century; and a Moorish-Burmese state since the tenth century.

Although the Russian people were deprived of all rights, they revolted en masse against the Polish occupation in the early seventeenth century, and again when called upon by Peter the Great to save the Holy Russian homeland from the Swedes before the Battle of Poltava in the early eighteenth century. Russia, one of the most backward countries in Europe, and supposedly pre-national, has confronted the national forces raised by revolutionary France with no less national fervor.[16]

The fact is that, even today – despite economic prosperity, a high standard of living, and economic globalization processes – the phenomenon of nationalism is also intensifying. The disintegration of Yugoslavia into nations, the desire of many Quebecers to leave the Canadian Federation, the desire of the Catalans to leave Spain are only partial evidence of the intensity of nationalist and ethnic sentiments that provoke inconsistency with economic logic, and often even contradict it. Indeed, it is clear that it is impossible to explain the fervor that nationalism evokes, the intense commitment that so many people feel toward their national identity, in ordinary economic and political terms. Only religion, because of its powerful symbolism and collective worship, can be a source of inspiration for such fervor.

Nationalism, according to scholars, is related to feelings of the "religious kind".[17] This is not a simplistic extension according to which nationalism is nothing but a "political religion", but is undoubtedly rooted in a deep consciousness of the sacred expressed in symbols common to the group as such. Charisma is an expression or representation of this sacred experience – a kind of totem that represents its power, for the specific collective.

From this angle, the charismatic person is, as stated, also an agent of the accumulated symbols of the group, representing a promise of power that has a quasi-eternal quality. In other words, the surprising power of the charismatic leader is achieved out of a longing for the ability (even if imagined) to mediate to us through our sensitivity, a promise inherent in us. As complex as the charismatic message may be, it has the simple, but super-temporal, experiential quality similar to that of a mother taking a baby in her arms – a sense of "coming home".

Charisma, according to this notion, is never the thing itself (a communicative interaction between an authority figure and its recipients), but the latent power it represents. The surprising quality of a charismatic performance does not stem from the "charismatic" figure (always flesh and blood) or his message in itself, but from the greater thing it represents for us: a strong promise toward which we are primed and ever-responsive – as part of the human race's "addiction" to symbols and to those who carry them and communicate them skillfully.

Such aspects of symbolic collective identity have been "inherited" and accelerated through "leadership meetings" within collectives, while empowering the collective and also distinguishing it from others in processes such as natural pedagogy. Observing the history and the role of the great figures within it, as accelerators of symbols and identities, clearly indicate this.[18] It is enough to read the Bible and constitutive theological texts to see the centrality of charismatic leaders.

Along these lines, certain publics are essentially "communities of emotion" that originate in a shared collective memory, and intensify the sense of family brotherhood. Indeed, an analysis of the rhetoric of leaders – and strikingly, the more charismatic ones[19] – indicates frequent use of "family terms", which provides a vital psychic connection. Similarly, the rhetoric of nationalism is fundamentally popular and ethnic. Nationalism is a manifestation of both: the individual universal need of human beings, as well as separate ethnic groups with a unique history and culture that usually resides in a particular ancestral territory.[20]

From this perspective, one can point to many examples of charismatic leaders who actually form the focus of the feelings inherent in the sense of brotherhood built within a collective in a long historical process. That is, the leader is often not the actual person who embodies those qualities that seemingly indicate salient abilities, but a myth built out of public desires. A notable example of this is the story of Joan of Arc from the more mythological leadership in French history. This is a girl who was executed at the age of 19. She was illiterate and was never trained in military affairs. So, the question is: How could such a young and incompetent girl become a leader on a national scale? It is clear that this is a myth – a story built on the processes of canonization that created collective solidarity.[21]

Joan of Arc, in today's terms, was suspected of schizophrenia (she heard voices) and certainly would not have been given military forces to command as the French King Charles did. It should be noted that Charles, himself, suffered glorious failures at the hands of the British and fought for his very coronation. His willingness to allow Joan of Arc to "play military games" is completely incomprehensible and was probably a move stemming from his own dismal situation, along with various pressures from a desperate and bitter population. However, Joan of Arc's victories (which were partial and limited) over the English were in small guerrilla battles aimed at the vulnerability of the British – a kind of fighting that was not acceptable at that time. These small battles came after a long series of defeats in huge face-to-face battles against the English, and became a source of national pride that had been sorely lacking.

Thus, it seems that the story created around Joan of Arc served the "large family" (the French collective) in its desire to promote a sense of collective brotherhood that has, as discussed, cultural-evolutionary roots.

The example of Nazi Germany provides an opportunity to examine this claim in a much more thorough and empirical way than the mythological story of a young girl-turned-leader during the fifteenth century's Hundred Years' War.

First, let's look at the German "combustible materials", as suggested, through the perspective offered by the nationalism researcher, Anthony Smith,[22] and try to explain the sources of the national fervor, which is clearly related to the leaders who both represent and incite the group.

The idea of "heroic" leadership was part of German historical development, part of the collective memory passed down from generation to generation. Bismarck worship, pretentious images of imperial splendor and military glory, acceptance of the authority of a "great leader", who would revive the heroic and mythical past values that would ensure the resurrection of the nation, were ingrained in German discourse in all its ramifications.[23]

This cultural element served as an accelerating force during the crisis (which, as discussed, activates phylogenetic tendencies to seek large figures), since the inherent images of heroic leadership were in contrast to the image of the unimpressive party activists quarreling in the Reichstag.

Writer, Ernest Junger, saw the "great politician of the future" as a "modern man of power" in the "machine era" – "a man of outstanding intelligence", perhaps emerging from a party, but standing "above parties and divisions", whose natural instinct and will would select the right path and overcome all obstacles.[24]

The journalist, Wilhelm Stappel, published a well-known essay depicting the figure of the "true leader" as "ruler, warrior and priest" at the same time. Staple's essay gives expression to a secular belief in redemption wrapped in imaginary religious language. It seems that the Germans were, perhaps more than any other Western culture, close to the ideas of the Scottish philosopher, Carlyle, from the Romantic philosophical stream that believed "history is but a biography of leaders".[25]

As noted by nationalism scholar, Anthony Smith,[26] religious symbolism has a profound emotional effect. Acceptable analyses of culture – made on the basis of folklore analysis, texts, plays, and rhetoric – indeed point to the existing theological foundation in the context of Hitler's growth as a charismatic leader.

This element in German culture was exemplified in the analysis of Faustic folklore staged by Johann Wolfgang Goethe.[27] Goethe's play expresses all the important motifs in the discussion of permeating codes and influences, as reflected in German culture. In the play's prologue, one already sees a different conception of divinity than that described in the Scriptures. God is depicted as a ridiculous, old, troubled entity, with the much more impressive figure of the Devil (Mephisto) beside him.

In Goethe's prologue, God is portrayed as bored in the company of his good angels, who utter words of praise for his ears. He prefers his naughty son Mephisto. Of Jesus there is no trace in the prologue. The Devil is the only impressive character in the play. God sends Mephisto to spur lazy humanity on to be more active. Unlike stories that appear in the myths of different religions, there is no message here about redemption, hope, mercy, or love. There is only a message about an *act*.

Dr. Faust, the protagonist of Goethe's drama – the man who makes a pact with the Devil – lived during the Reformation and was an alchemist who practiced magic. He was purported to have supernatural powers. He did not want to continue to be bound by moral debates which demanded his restraint. On the contrary, he aspired to start his life anew. He wanted deeds!

Faust makes a pact with the Devil to achieve his maximum pleasures and to receive supernatural powers from him. For a moment, he is willing to ignore his fear of the Devil, who is about to take ownership of his soul in payment for the pleasures he has given him. This is a decision that could not have been deduced from most of the well-known religious stories (which, as mentioned, are sources of moral or hopeful messages). The religious archetype is consistent with the way human consciousness works. This recognition presents the conclusion that everything has a price.

There are variations among different religions and cultures regarding the *form* of payment – some emphasize asceticism, some make sacrifices to please the gods, and some connect the sacrifice with redemption (in the Catholic Mass, for example, the participant taking part in the public prayer is supposedly sacrificed together with Jesus and then redeemed with him). Here, in Goethe's drama, Faust signs a pact with the Devil, but also evades payment and wins the "fun" part of the deal without having to give up his soul in return.

This story could have been referred to as another marginal insignificant story, which might interest literary and folklore scholars. The fact is, however, that the myth of Faust affected German creators and artists in a way that is unique to Germany. For example, the great German writer, Thomas Mann, who left Germany following the intensification of Nazism, sharply saw the cultural connection between Faust, Luther, and the rise of Hitler. At least 20 versions have been made from the Faust myth in Germany, including musical versions. Moreover, this myth, which was received with such great enthusiasm in Germany, was not met with acceptance or praise elsewhere. In England, for example, the play elicited responses of contempt, rejection, and disgust.[28]

Indeed, there is an extensive body of literature that discusses leadership as a cultural phenomenon. As the Dutch scholar, Geert Hofstede, put it: "Beliefs about leaders represent a dominant cultural component in a given society or country. Asking people about the qualities of leaders who are good in their eyes is like describing their culture. The leader is a cultural hero."[29] "Culture", as described in the second chapter, is a kind of genetic code. Everyone recognizes its importance and centrality, even though it does not have the same type of "concrete reality" that allows biologists to study a genetic code. Regarding the reference to leaders, this cultural code is an addition to the universal tendencies described previously: the need for a large figure, who is competent and caring. In other words, the need for a leader (which is universal) has different expressions among different collectives. This, of course, is reflected in the stories and mythologies that are learned and passed down from generation to generation. These stories naturally have an impact on people growing up in their light.

By framing the discussion of the influence of charismatic leaders as a dynamic of "neediness and greatness", we can argue that most of the German public had a cultural longing for a great heroic leader of the practical kind (as embodied in the Faustian myth). This insight makes it possible to more clearly analyze the question posed by the British historian, Ian Kershaw, who devoted 20 years of his life to the riddle of Hitler's charisma, saying,

> How do we explain how someone with so few intellectual gifts and social attributes, someone no more than an empty vessel outside his political life, unapproachable and impenetrable even for those in his close company, incapable it seems of genuine friendship, without the background that bred high office, without even any experience of government before becoming Reich Chancellor, could nevertheless have such an immense historical impact, could make the entire world hold its breath?[30]

There is perhaps no charismatic leader who has been written about as much as Hitler. From all that has been written, if one compares this body of work to most biographies of well-known leaders, there is no evidence in Hitler's childhood and adolescence that hints that he was destined for leadership. In fact, it is doubtful that he even had the motivation for it. In his youth, he wanted to be an artist, a painter. How did a man who did not believe in his own ability to lead become the most famous charismatic leader of the modern age?

This is an important and fascinating story because it provides insights into the question: How is "greatness" created?, especially in the eyes of the needy, as described.

The first angle for examining this issue is the leader's reference to himself. Winston Churchill, for example, believed wholeheartedly from his youth that he was destined for greatness – to save Britain. This belief was not only a matter of destiny, Churchill believed in his ability to perform this role better than others (the title of a well-known biography of Churchill accurately expresses this: *A Study in Greatness*[31]).

Similar lines can be found in the biographies of other prominent charismatic leaders, who often grew up in conditions that allowed them to see themselves from an early age as those destined for leadership. This includes the likes of Franklin Roosevelt, David Ben-Gurion, Ata Turk, Nelson Mandela, Mahatma Gandhi, and many others. From a young age, they found themselves in leadership positions and influential roles that felt natural to them because of their self-perception and personality.[32]

This, however, was not the case with Hitler. In his self-image as a young man, there was not the slightest hint of his perceiving himself as a leader. Even in the post-World War I years, the liberated Hitler, the Corporal with the Iron Cross decoration (which greatly benefited him later), lived in Munich in a neglected apartment, spent his time and vented his rage among fringe circles, which met in beer cellars and mourned Germany's decline.

At one of these meetings held in 1919, Hitler sought to respond to a speech that had angered him. It was the first time he spoke publicly, despite the opposition of members of the secretariat who doubted his talents. When he started speaking, he surprised everyone with an emotional speech that lasted 30 minutes. He described his feelings about this speech in his book *Mein Kampf*: "I spoke for 30 minutes. And something that I always felt deep down in my heart, without really knowing, was here proven to be true: I could speak! After my 30 minutes, the people in the little hall were electrified. Their enthusiasm found its first expression in the fact that my appeal to those present brought us donations of 300 marks."[33]

The effect of being able to speak with excitement, enthusiasm, to affect others' emotions, was soon discovered. Being "up on stage" ignited in Hitler the desire and ability to move the audience. His on-stage persona was different from his usual personality. On stage, the refined and ultimate struggle of admiration took place – a distinctly narcissistic motif that appears in the lives of many well-known actors.[34]

This motivational aspect is probably one of the important distinctions between charismatic leaders such as Lincoln, Franklin Roosevelt, Ben Gurion, Mahatma Gandhi, and Nelson Mandela, who are considered "positive charismatics", and leaders like Hitler and Jim Jones who are considered "negative charismatics".

The former all had a positive self-image. Most of those mentioned above, as noted, perceived themselves as destined for leadership and suited to it from the beginning. The latter discovered their ability to influence others under random circumstances that summoned them to a stage. Indeed, if there is an element that is common in the analysis of their biographies, it is the huge gap between the feelings of loneliness and neglect they experienced in childhood, and the admiration they received on stage. Real addiction patterns can be identified in these displays of charisma. Some even explicitly stated this. Without the admiration of the audience, there was no purpose to their lives.[35]

As noted in the opening chapter, even after his talent for rhetoric was revealed, Hitler still did not see himself as a "great leader". As mentioned, he defined his role at this point as a "drummer", calling on the masses to come follow the great leader. The "heroic leadership" that Hitler claimed for himself (after being imprisoned) was, in fact, the invention of his loyalists even before he saw himself in that position. However, the role suited the temperament of a man who – because of his personal failures in his early life – found excessive satisfaction in an admiration that knew no bounds. This combination of admiration for heroes showered on him by others, together with Hitler's inability to see his own flaws and errors, created in his narcissistic personality a formidable self-image of "heroic leadership".[36]

Indeed, in *Mein Kampf* Hitler portrayed himself as a mighty genius whose personality combined the qualities of a "programmatic" and a "Politician". The "programmatic" is a theorist who deals with "eternal truths" as the great religious leaders did. The "greatness" of the "Politician" is reflected in the successful implementation of the "idea" devised by the "programmatic". "Over long periods of humanity," he wrote, "it can once happen that the politician is wedded to the programmatic." His work did not concern short-term demands that any petty bourgeois could grasp, but looked to the future, with "aims which only the fewest grasp"... "the combination of theoretician, organizer, and leader in one person is the rarest thing that can be found on this earth; this combination makes the great man".[37]

This self-conviction, deep as it may be, would of course have been of no real value if it had not come into contact with such flammable fuel. The Nazi party knowingly and actively became a "movement of a leader", focused both ideologically and organizationally on Hitler's cult. Rudolf Hess, a supporter of Hitler for many years, saw the cult of the leader as a matter of deep faith, even a psychological need. In a letter to Walter Wall, later one of Ribbentrop's chief aides at the State Department, Hess mentions the "leadership principle" outlined by Hitler: "unconditional authority downwards, and responsibility upwards". He calls it "Germanic democracy". At the end of the letter, he likens the "the great popular leader" to "the great founder of a religion". His task is not to consider the pros and cons like an academic, and not to allow himself the freedom to think there is another truth. "He must communicate to his listeners an apodictic faith. Only then can the mass of followers be led where they should be led. They will then also follow the leader if setbacks are encountered." [38]

Even people who were critical of Hitler's personality and did not see themselves as his admirers, such as Gregory Strasser (a senior member of the Nazi party, who was assassinated on the Night of the Long Knives in 1934), were convinced that the Fuhrer cult had to be cultivated to preserve the unity embodied in the figure of the leader. The "Heil Hitler" salute, wrote Strasser in January 1927, is not only a symbol of personal dependence on the leader, but contains within itself an oath of allegiance to an ancient relationship that is both aristocratic and democratic, between the leader and his followers.

Not only analyses of well-known people about the German-like religious tradition inherent in heroic leadership attest to a cultural spirit. This is mainly evidenced by the countless quotations of simple people in whom the spark powerfully ignited the ideals which were instilled in them. One of the war veterans said that his admiration for Hitler began when he listened to his speeches: "He evoked the feelings of every good German. The German soul spoke to German manhood in his words. From that day on I could never violate my allegiance to Hitler. I saw his unlimited faith in his people and the desire to set them free."[39]

As is well known, millions of Germans shared this feeling. These basic positions were later actively nurtured by Hitler's loyalists, who saw his deification as a powerful means of strengthening control and unity. First and foremost among them was Goebbels, who used a mystical language that was rooted in German romanticism and spoke specifically to the pre-Nazi youth movement. In a pamphlet written by him, Hitler is described as "the fulfilment of a mysterious longing", bringing faith in deepest despair, "a meteor before our astonished eyes", working "a miracle of enlightenment and belief in a world of skepticism and despair".[40]

The association with religious rallies in churches and in various mystical circles is inevitable. Indeed, like any phenomenon that is exciting and laden with emotions – even if it is associated with blatantly secular figures – its enthusiastic expression has "religious" characteristics. This is a passion that had early origins. Observing the phenomenon of charisma through the metaphor of fire seems to be striking and helpful. A careful analysis makes it clear that those who determine the height of the flame and how long it will last are the combustibles. If they are not flammable enough, even if the fire is lit, the flame will go out in a short time; and it will be even shorter if there is no oxygen feeding it.

According to this view, the most important sources of charisma are those same elements that have been described as inherent in the followers – their innate tendencies, as demonstrated in the pedagogical learning studies, and their cultural biases. Charisma, as described, is more a manifestation of the followers than a characteristic of the leader.

This observation is gaining increasing expression in empirical studies that attempt to identify and follow those variables that explain the attractiveness of charismatics of all kinds. For example, Danish researchers examined brain responses that were thought to be influenced by the degree of charisma of a pastor who delivered a sermon in a church.[41]

Two groups listened to the pastor: a group of devout religious Christians who saw the pastor as a charismatic figure by virtue of his status, by being a "messenger of God", and a secular group that did not at all see the pastor as a charismatic figure with the powers attributed to him by the first group. The researchers found that in the group of religious believers, there was a significant degree of de-activation of the social executive functions in the brain – an effect similar to that of hypnosis on the brain. That is, the cerebral activity indicates that the religious group relinquished control and alertness and "surrendered" to the leader, in contrast to the other (secular) group, whose degree of cerebral activity in those parts of the brain actually increased. These findings are consistent with Wilson and Sperber's well-known theory of relevance,[42] according to which people have different "relevance thresholds". When people are exposed to information, once they find relevant meaning for them that calms their "adaptive stress", the processing of new information is weakened or ceases altogether, and the meaning of the additional things loses relevance.

Processing charisma as signals is probably also subject to a similar pattern. We surrender and synchronize when the leadership messages are close to our symbolic center, that is, jumping quickly, when it comes to the "sacred" symbols of the family, our sports team, and so on compared to less interest in the symbols of others. Indeed, our perception of the influence of significant others around us is subject to various levels of relevance – the most prominent of which are related to the cultural relevance described as being itself subject to developments that began as grouping processes in human evolution.

This perspective gives us an observational lens that allows for an analysis of the questions posed at the beginning of the book: Why are leaders who are charismatic in one group not necessarily perceived as being charismatic in the eyes of another group?

As we have seen, there are cultural differences among groups. These differences are evident in many ways. For example, Americans relate to time as a resource that has a value which must be well utilized (time is money). This is not the case in some South American cultures, where time does not have the same value, certainly not economic value. The attitude to work or success as shown by Max Weber is also related to religious and cultural foundations. Protestants, he claims, treat success at work differently than Catholics. The significant success of Jews in certain fields was explained by a pair of economists through a historical-cultural analysis of the values Jews were careful to pass on from generation to generation.[43] In short, if "cultural baggage" is so valuable in explaining consistent responses and behaviors regarding various aspects of daily life, why should it not be the same for leaders, regarding their choice and followers' willingness to comply to them?

We will now summarize the general conceptual framework: the most basic and universal explanation for humans' longing for charismatic leaders and responses to them is related to signals of *competence and caring* – just as in the example presented about animals living in groups.

The figure experienced as powerful in the adaptive struggle (competence) will have more odds of being granted leadership. But his status will not last if he does not share the spoils with the others (signals of generosity and care). This equation is constantly being scrutinized by followers. This is an ongoing validation of the trust granted to leaders without which leaders have no influence.

The most universal expression of this argument is most clearly expressed in crisis situations. (Psychoanalysts, for example, will characterize this as a regression to early phases of development.) Whatever the explanation, it is a situation to which responses are anchored in a clear evolutionary logic, as John Bowlby showed in his well-known attachment theory.[44]

While the signs of competence and caring are especially prominent in crisis situations – during which the existential circumstantial component is undeniable – there is ample evidence of their centrality in other circumstances as well. For example, in most recognized election campaigns in the West, certain variables such as experience (which usually involves older age) carry a lot of weight.

Together with this the acquired cultural signals will have a particular impact on the intensity of the attraction to leaders – the "height of the flames" and its duration. As we have shown, there are groups in which the collective memory has nurtured the myths of heroic leaders; on the other hand, there are groups in which such myths have not been nurtured.[45]

The claim regarding the intergenerational transmission of cultural norms is significant in understanding the generalizability of "signals of charisma". Of particular importance is the homogeneity of the group. It is clear that the more homogeneous the group (i.e., the more shared commonalities members have such as a common language, symbols, and rituals passed down from generation to generation), the more similar the response to displayed signals will be. Germany, during the period analyzed in this chapter, is an example of a society with a relatively high level of homogeneity. On the other hand, immigrant societies like Canada, the United States, or Australia are made up of different immigrant groups who have brought with them different cultures. Therefore, the discussion about them in the context of attraction to leaders is more complex.[46]

Indeed, in the election of leaders in countries with high immigration levels, there is a great expression of ethnicity. It is not for nothing that journalists and political scientists talk about terma such as "politics of identities". This concept clearly contains cultural-ethnic differences that have an expression in the choice of leaders. In our case, they represent different (acquired) signs of charisma.

We would like to reiterate that *signals* of leadership trigger emotions. Charisma, as noted at the beginning of the chapter, is not some "trick" that the leader exercises independently of his environment. To a large extent, the leader's influence is conditioned by those values and needs which are relevant to the group. Based on these arguments, it is important to distinguish between the universal and the local-cultural in the study of charisma. A central challenge in analyzing charismatic leaders is to discern when signs of charisma are more universal, that is, related to primary human needs, or when they are more culturally dependent. This is probably the most complex part of the discussion.

Either way, according to our argument, charisma as we have described it here is an emotional, rapid influence that "emerges" because of our specific biological and symbolic readiness. As such, charisma is related to an unconscious developmental purpose that exists, for the most part, at the group level rather than the individual level. This collective readiness emerges, like a kind of evolutionary engine, which then harnesses itself to the front of the train and pulls it toward its goal: turning individuals into coordinated groups, even though we, the passengers on the train, may have the illusory feeling that we are "behind the wheel". Thus, at this level of analysis, one can understand the inexplicably "magical" experience of charisma, as well as the potential threat which lurks within.

NOTES

1. Allison, Scott T. and Goethals, George R. (2011). *Heroes: What They Do and Why We Need Them*. New York: Oxford University Press.
2. Popper, Micha (2001). *Hypnotic Leadership*. Westport, CT, Praeger.
3. Bailly, Jean-Sylvian (2002). Secret Report on Mesmerism or Animal Magnetism. *International Journal of Clinical and Experimental Hypnosis*, 50(4) (October), 364–8.
4. Popper, *Hypnotic Leadership*, p. 9.
5. Hasson, Uri, Ghazanfar, Asif A., Galantucci, Bruno, Garrod, Simon, and Keysers, Christian (2012). Brain-to-brain coupling: A mechanism for creating and sharing a social world. *Trends in Cognitive Sciences*, 16(2), 114–21.
6. Shteynberg, Garriy (2010). A silent emergence of culture: The social tuning effect. *Journal of Personality and Social Psychology*, 99(4), 683.
7. Feldman, R. (2007). Parent–infant synchrony and the construction of shared timing; physiological precursors, developmental outcomes, and risk conditions. *Journal of Child Psychology and Psychiatry*, 48(3–4), 329–54.

8.   Feldman, R., Magori-Cohen, R., Galili, G., Singer, M., and Louzoun, Y. (2011). Mother and infant coordinate heart rhythms through episodes of interaction synchrony. *Infant Behavior and Development*, 34(4), 569–77.

9.   Boyd, Robert and Richerson, Peter J. (2005). *The Origin and Evolution of Cultures*. Oxford: Oxford University Press.

10. Grossmann, Tobias (2013). The role of medial prefrontal cortex in early social cognition. *Frontiers in Human Neuroscience*, 7, 340.

11. Schwartz, Barry (2000). *Abraham Lincoln. Forge of National Memory*. Chicago, IL: University of Chicago Press.

12. Antonakis, J., Bastardoz, N., Jacquart, P., and Shamir, B. (2016). Charisma: An ill-defined and ill-measured gift. *Annual Review of Organizational Psychology and Organizational Behavior*, 3, 293–319.

13. Popper, *Hypnotic Leadership*.

14. Gellner, Ernest (2006). *Nations and Nationalism*, 2nd edn. Ithaca, NY: Cornell University Press.

15. Gat, Azar (2013). *Nations: The Long History of Deep Roots of Political Ethnicity and Nationalism*. New York: Cambridge University Press. Smith, Anthony D. (1986). *The Ethnic Origins of Nations*. Oxford: Blackwell.

16. Gat, *Nations*.

17. Smith, *The Ethnic Origins of Nations*.

18. Ibid., p. 45.

19. Shamir, Boas, Michael B. Arthur, and Robert J. House (1994). The rhetoric of charismatic leadership: A theoretical extension, a case study and implications for research. *Leadership Quarterly*, 5(1), 25.

20. Connor, Walker (1994). *Ethno-Nationalism: The Quest of Understanding*. Princeton, NJ: Princeton University Press.

21. Popper, Micha and Castelnovo, Omri (2018). The function of great leaders in human culture: A cultural-evolutionary perspective. *Leadership*, 14(6), 757–74.

22. Smith, *The Ethnic Origins of Nations*.

23. Kershaw, Ian (1998). *Hitler, 1889–1936: Hubris*. London: Penguin Books.

24. Ibid., p. 181.

25. Carlyle, Thomas (1841), *On Heroes, Hero-Worship and the Heroic in History*, reprinted 1907. Boston: Houghton Mifflin.

26. Smith, *The Ethnic Origins of Nations*.

27. Shechter, Rivka (1990). *The Theological Foundations of the Third Reich*. Tel Aviv: Ministry of Defense Publishing (Hebrew).

28. Ibid.

29. Hofstede, Geert (1997). *Cultures and Organizations: The Software of the Mind*. New York: McGraw-Hill, p. 7.

30. Kershaw, *Hitler, 1889–1936*, p. xxiv.

31. Best, Geoffrey (2003). *Churchill: A Study in Greatness*. New York: Oxford University Press.

32. Popper, Micha (2012). *Fact and Fantasy about Leadership*. Cheltenham, UK and Northampton, MA, USA: Edward Elgar.

33. Hitler, Adolf (2018). *Mein Kampf* (Vol. 1), trans. Thomas Dalton. New York: Clemens and Blair, p. 352.

34. Popper, *Hypnotic Leadership*.
35. Ibid.
36. Kershaw, *Hitler, 1889–1936*, p. 251.
37. Ibid., pp. 251–2.
38. Ibid., pp. 294–5.
39. Ibid., p. 295.
40. Ibid., p. 295.
41. Schjoedt, Uffe, Stødkilde-Jørgensen, Hans, Geertz, Armin W., Lund, Torben E., and Roepstorff, Andreas (2010). The power of charisma: Perceived charisma inhibits the frontal executive network of believers in intercessory prayer. *Social Cognitive and Affective Neuroscience*, nsq023.
42. Wilson, Deirdre and Sperber, Dan (2012). *Meaning and Relevance*. Cambridge: Cambridge University Press.
43. Botticini, Maristella and Eckstein, Zvi (2012). *The Chosen Few: How Education Shaped Jewish History*. Princeton, NJ: Princeton University Press.
44. Bowlby, John (1973), *Attachment and Loss, Vol. 2: Separation*. New York: Basic Books.
45. Halbwachs, Maurice (1926/1950), *The Collective Memory*, reprinted 1950, trans. F.J. and V.Y. Ditter. London: Harper Colophon Books.
46. Popper, *Fact and Fantasy about Leadership*.

5. Reflections and unresolved questions

WHY ARE THERE LEADERS, AFTER ALL?

If, as described, the default mode according to evolutionary logic is to wish to be *a follower*, that is, to be protected by large figures and learn from them about ways to exist and thrive, then the following question arises: *Where do the leaders come from*? How is it that people continue to emerge from this "automatic pattern"? If followership is, indeed, the default mode, then what is it that makes some people want to be leaders?

This issue was not examined according to the theoretical basis presented in the book; however, explanations can be found in the biographies of charismatic leaders, in which the psychological sources underlying their development as leaders were examined. The findings are thought-provoking if one tries to interpret them according to the reasoning at the heart of the book.

For example, a perusal of some of the more reliable biographies of known charismatic leaders such as Mahatma Gandhi,[1] Nelson Mandela,[2] and Bill Clinton[3] suggests a loving relationship with the mother and the absence of a father figure. In such circumstances, the mother had expectations that the "good and capable boy" would take on some of the roles of the father. And so, such a child becomes a kind of parental figure who learns not only to internalize parental responsibility, but also to practice parental roles that are important antecedents of leadership.[4]

Indeed, there is evidence supporting the possibility that these are not exceptional cases that have no generalizability at all. While collecting material for the biographies of 24 British prime ministers – from Spencer Percival in 1809 to Neville Chamberlain in 1937 – British researcher, Lucille Iremonger,[5] was surprised to find that 15 of them, or 66 percent, had lost their father during childhood. A 1921 census revealed that in the general population, only 2 percent of children were orphans. A sample of 45 British CEOs who ran large companies found that nearly half of them had lost a father when they were under 16 and, as a result, were expected to take responsibility very early.[6] These expectations were internalized and became part of the motivation to play an influential role. A study with similar results was conducted among people who grew up during the Great Depression in the United States.[7] It was found that children whose father was unemployed during the crisis and, as a result, were exposed early to life's responsibilities and difficulties, tended in adulthood to seek managerial roles.

It should be emphasized that this pattern characterizes "positive charismatic leaders". This is not the case with "negative charismatic" leaders such as Hitler or Jim Jones who, as briefly described, experienced in many cases a childhood of neglect, sometimes violence, and marginality. No expectations to achieve leadership roles were radiated toward them, and they were not trained for it. Their leadership was – as can be interpreted from the psychological similarities of their childhood – the fruit of a random revelation that became an addiction to the attention and adoration of others: compensation for narcissistic deprivation.[8]

The positive charismatic leaders had opportunities to build confidence based on early experience of key elements of "leadership work". This combination created in them the ability to be less dependent on external confirmations of their value and to have a stronger sense of emotional security. This is reflected in the signals' dynamics, which enhances trust in its most fundamental form among followers: competence and care. Meaning, the signal is: "I know what to do and I care about you."[9]

In the case of the negative charismatic leaders, narcissistic deprivation may lead to an excessive preoccupation with intra-psychic processes, possibly accompanied by delusions of grandeur that leave no room for others' needs. The focus of the effort is derived from the need to compensate for past injuries and neglect. True, trust in a negative charismatic leader can indeed arise quickly, but its real test is over time, so the invalidity of the relationship is exposed along the way, especially in the context of the generosity factor. The demands for constant admiration can crash rapidly and dramatically reduce the followers' trust.[10]

The outlines of such an observation have been extensively discussed in the psychodynamic literature dealing with leadership. But the adoption of elements that have an evolutionary rationale can extend the discussion to levels of generalizability that are beyond the biographical story of a particular leader.

John Bowlby's theory,[11] anchored in an evolutionary assumption, can illustrate the expanded perspective in such an analysis, and provide a more generalizable answer regarding the distinction between negative charismatic leaders and positive charismatic leaders.

As mentioned, in accordance with Bowlby's attachment theory, immense importance is attributed to the initial bond formed between the infant and the caregiver. The emotional impact formed during this period (the "internal working model" in attachment theory terms) serves as a "compass", which guides emotional relationships in adulthood. One of the patterns that develops as a result of the caregiver's insensitivity, neglect, and indifference is defined as an "avoidant pattern". Its essence, in the context in question, is the ability to distance emotions and rely less on others. In some cases, it will be difficult for someone who is characterized as "avoidant" to properly assess feelings and social situations. This, of course, has implications regarding the dynamics of trust in general,[12] and in the context of the leader–follower relationship, in particular.

However, in the context discussed, from the followers' perspective, this type of avoidant pattern can create attributions of power that serve their need for "greatness". For example, Charles Manson, Jim Jones, and Hitler were perceived as figures whose power was such that they did not need the "ordinary things" that ordinary people need. They were perceived as beings who are above "such trifles". This image was necessary for the followers because of their own needs. Had the followers known about the internal conflicts and fragility of their leaders, their charisma would have been shattered. These are extreme, but clear, examples which illustrate the argument that charisma is not just a possible impressive image in the eyes of the followers; in some cases, it is simply a distorted creation of their projections and attributions.

IN WHAT WAY DOES HUMAN LEADERSHIP DIFFER FROM THAT OF OTHER ANIMALS?

Reflection: One day in the summer of 2019, a terrible incident occurred. A man was murdered in the city of Ramla in a parking lot in front of his wife and daughters because he asked another car owner to move his car over a little bit, so that he could park too. What added to the horror was the fact that the murdered man (whom the killer did not even know) was the mainstay of a family with disabled children.[13]

This case has raised many questions. First of all, the killer was a 74-year-old man, completely normative, with no criminal record, and a clean personal and occupational history. So, why did this happen? Answering this question calls for an interesting observation, according to which manifestations of brutal violence appear more frequently in crowded places in which there are constant feelings of stress. Hours of traffic jams, queues everywhere including restaurants and beaches, endless, obsessive searches for parking, and so on – all culminate in a constant feeling not only of having to be alert and competitive at all times, but the feeling that without a certain amount of aggression you will most likely "come out a sucker". In short, living under stressful conditions may be often accompanied by the feeling that it is "either me or them". The supply is always smaller than the demand.

Isn't this a primary feeling shared by all living creatures in a world of many threats and limited opportunities? Isn't this the shared experience of our forefathers, who sought sources of livelihood while making a daily attempt to stay alive? That is, living in threatening places is perhaps an environment clearly associated with the earliest evolutionary environment. Might it be true that the idea "more violent cultures" is merely a derivative of the equation of threats and opportunities?[14]

Some highlight the uniqueness of humans, claiming that when they feel they are moving away from existential danger, humans can be less associated with instincts needed so badly to the struggle for existence and security – the two basic stages in Maslow's famous hierarchy of needs.[15] Then, as Maslow claims, Man will be able to address social matters and climb up the ladder to "self-fulfillment" – aspects that are culture-bound.

Maslow's distinction was also used to analyze collectives. American sociologist, Ron Ingelhart,[16] distinguishes between societies guided by materialist values and societies guided by post-materialist values. *Materialist values* include existence and security, while *post-materialist* values are values related to the environment and quality of life.

Societies in the material stage are societies in which most of the energy is still directed toward physical existence, and reflect the conditions of survival described in the early stages of evolutionary development. It can be said, as Hofstede[17] argued, that the comparison between different societies is, in fact, a comparison of cultures. A central aspect of such comparisons is reflected in what leaders represent. Is it possible, as noted, to understand Mahatma Gandhi's rise to the status of India's leader and his subsequent transformation into a myth of leadership, without understanding Hindu culture? Can the mythological story built around the leadership of the most revered American president, Abraham Lincoln, be understood and interpreted as such in a non-American culture? It seems clear to all that Gandhi – because of his dress, manners, and values –

would not have been chosen as a leader in the United States. Most likely, culturally he would have been perceived as stranger.

Indeed, the discussion in the literature is, to a great extent, dichotomous: according to the "existential" understanding, the leader is the coordinating function of the group's actions. The better the coordination is, the better the group's chances of survival.[18] According to the "cultural" understanding, the leader is the focal point of the group's identity. His being a catalyst of psychological, social, and cultural processes is the frame of reference for much research and analysis.[19]

As argued in the opening chapter of the book, these perspectives reduce or create arbitrary categories regarding human nature. There is a tendency, as pointed out by Ernest Becker,[20] to see human nature as having one constitutive essence at a given point in time.

The idea that human beings (sometimes at the same time) are "both" biological and symbolic creatures is difficult to digest, and certainly for analysis and interpretation in a world whose analytical tools are disciplinary (the divisions of scientific journals are the clearest illustration of this).

Becker demonstrates the complexity and validity of the "both argument", through a brilliant analysis of human attitudes toward death. This angle of observation makes it possible to clearly see both aspects. The uniqueness of humans lies in this combination. As Becker argues, Man throughout his life must constantly choose between two decisive choices: to be an animal or to be an angel. The difficulties and complexities resulting from this choice stem from the existence of both elements and humans' need to live with both.

All animals, including humans, want to survive and reproduce. To do so, as discussed, they develop abilities which improve the practice of survival and reproduction. However, there are some significant differences between humans and other animals. One of them is the reference to death. Only Man is aware of his certain end. This knowledge accompanies him throughout most of his life (and intensifies in his later years). In fact, Becker argues, for most of a person's life, he is preoccupied, to one degree or another, with various configurations in denying the meaning of this awareness, but this is also a tremendous driving force, even if it is not always at the center of consciousness.

Prominent sculptors, musicians, and painters who were childless claimed that "their works are their children". Their works are, in fact, their legacy for future generations. In other words, symbolic death is not subject to the limitations of biological death. The rhetoric at funerals and memorials clearly expresses this feeling: "Their memory will not vanish"; "They will remain in our hearts" ... Man has a symbolic life as well as symbolic desires that somehow help to deny the finitude of life, or at least give a comforting meaning to death. Our various works (including our descendants) are the promise that we will not disappear completely after our physical demise. This perspective helps to interpret some key aspects presented in the book regarding leadership and followership.

First, the distinction between the existential or the "animal" part and the "symbolic" part is probably overly simplistic and certainly narrow. Evolutionary logic illuminates the adaptive stages and their nature. As shown, the understanding that the adaptively significant unit of existence is the group – from family to large groups – clarifies that it is, in fact, a sequence of evolutionary development of which the symbolic component is a part. Boyd, Richerson, and Henrich[21] describe this combination of the biological and the symbolic as a unique adaptation of the human race, as a niche of which culture plays a part. The development of language and the symbolic amount of information humans had to process; the development of complex collaboration skills; and the ability to learn and pass on methods, practices, and tools – such as handling fire, cooking, and use of weapons – all created demands that affected our biology (e.g., cortex development and management functions), to create a niche that is biological just as it is cultural. Therefore, the dichotomous idea that culture and biology are "at war" over the control of human behavior is meaningless.

Very early in ontogenetic development (the development of the individual after birth), our biology accelerates us to enter the cultural field: to acquire language, understand symbols, be part of a group – "us" versus "them" – and to learn effectively and quickly from others (natural pedagogy). And so, we are shaped as biological-symbolic animals, within our cultural evolutionary niche. Therefore, it is very difficult to determine whether leadership is more of an evolutionary and universal development or a cultural and local development. The appropriate question to ask is *how* the interaction – between the primary, universal, genetic, and cultural elements – creates leadership and followership manifestations.

This direction can clarify, for example, what is behind our joy and frustration when our football team wins or loses. Or explain the reason for our tears when our national anthem is played or why our heart begins to beat more quickly when our flag is raised in public events. Such responses reflect our evolutionary need for grouping, cooperation (inward), caution, and sometimes hostility (outward), as we actively and restlessly seek content: a local flag, as well as a leader with whom we can feel part of a group, part of a family.

Indeed, one of the most significant distinctions that exists between humans and other animals concerns the ability to use symbols. A clear expression of this is, of course, the language through which meanings can be created that help coordination – the function that has been described as fundamental in the evolutionary struggle.

Symbols have great motivating power. They preserve an identity that is the basis for group solidarity. As any combat military unit knows, its beret, the unit's battle heritage stories, and other similar symbols contribute to the unit's solidarity, which has a clear existential meaning: just as romantic love is not only flowers, guitars, moonlight, and love songs, but a phenomenon that has primary sources of attraction,[22] biological-evolutionary aspects and symbolic aspects are intertwined.

Paraphrasing the well-known Clausewitz saying that "war is a continuation of politics by other means" it can be argued that the processes of symbolism and identity, group and culture involve the use of new sophisticated means for the existence and preservation of ancient goals. Leaders are one of the more central means of maintaining group threads.[23]

The speeches of great leaders in history well illustrate the value of symbolism for strengthening group solidarity. Winston Churchill's most famous speech, "Blood, Toil, Tears and Sweat"; Lincoln's Gettysburg Address; and other wartime speeches are spectacular demonstrations of symbols that enhance collective solidarity.

It is not for nothing that these speeches became canonical elements in history. They were delivered during times of crisis and struggle – times that empower leaders, who provide a symbolic answer, a way to cope during the struggle.

In this sense, there is a learned symbolic element in all human cultures. Intergenerational learning occurs through platforms like natural pedagogy, as described, which transfers the learner to another "state of aggregation": awakening, as it were, within us a "dormant giant" and turning us into a collective – a single link in a long and continuous cultural sequence. This is a universal process. However, the content carried on these platforms differs from collective to collective.

Natural pedagogy exists in all human groups. Cultural norms and practices are passed down from generation to generation in processes of imitation and internalization that always take place between large figures and small figures, who have great faith in the large figures. *This is a universal learning process.*

However, as shown by Max Weber and subsequent researchers, the degree of influence of the transmitted content is related to adaptation to changing environments. The evolutionary paradigm that provided insights into many phenomena has not been exhausted when it comes to such a central phenomenon as leadership.

Beyond the classifications discussed throughout the book, a fundamental element in the context of leadership, inherent in all human beings, is *trust*. Trust is the variable that pushes voters to vote for a particular leader, pushes soldiers to follow their commander into battle, and motivates employees to make extra efforts at the request of their superior. In fact, this is the driving force underlying any manifestation of acts that are "above and beyond" the call of duty. Identifying the factors that establish and increase trust is actually the core concern of all those involved in practicing and studying leadership.

In this sense, the book's discussion about signals of competence, caring, personal example, and attachment to group symbols is, in fact, a discussion about signals of trust and humans' sensitivity to such signals.

Therefore, to sum up, we focus on the issue of "formation of trust in the leader". The integrative quality of such a discussion can help create what researcher, Chris Argyris, called[24] "actionable knowledge" – conceptual knowledge that has practical implications.

Many theories make explicit or implicit assumptions about the "nature of humans" (e.g., good or bad). The evolutionary paradigm, as it is focused on adaptive learning and responsiveness to the environment, is more empirical in this sense. That is, humans respond and create patterns according to the conditions that the environment demands or summons. Different environments will activate different sensitivities and modes of response including the quality and duration of trust granting. We will now expand upon the foundations of trust in leaders.

ON TRUST IN THE LEADER

Studies on fraud, as well as dozens of instructive examples cited by Malcolm Gladwell,[25] illustrate the claim that granting trust is the default of most people. The analysis of the fraudulent act considered to be the greatest in the history of fraud, that of Bernie Madoff, points to this default. For example, several financial journalists as well as stockbrokers expressed that Madoff's conduct, and especially the sums of billions of dollars handled by him, aroused their suspicion. One of them even met with Madoff and years later said that it was almost impossible to sit with him there and believe he was a complete crook. He thought at the time that if he's running a Ponzi scheme, then either he's the best actor or he's a complete sociopath. He was very relaxed, almost as if the interview amused him. He came with a sort of attitude of "What sensible person could doubt me?"[26]

Such examples highlight the fact that even people who are supposed to be good at identifying crooks – because it is part of their job, are also influenced by a tendency to trust, rather than be suspicious. This default can clarify, for example, why people insist on repeatedly voting for "stars of the moment", who seem to pop up again and again in election campaigns, without checking too much. In fact, people invest less thought in choosing leaders who may determine their fate than in choosing a car or a home – decisions which, as described, utilize System 2 thinking, which involves analyzing data and scrutinizing it thoroughly.

This is the place to once again mention the important distinction between distant leaders (e.g., political leaders) and close leaders – leaders in daily life: in organizations, in the community, in social groups. This distinction is relevant to the issue of trust in leaders. As we have shown, the signals related to close leaders are more behavioral (e.g., personal example), while the signals related to distant leaders are more symbolic. In fact, it is easier for followers to validate their tendency to trust close leaders by relating to clear criteria such as: Does he (the leader) set a personal example? Do the leader's decisions take the group into account? Does the leader exhibit signals of caring, and so on. Since the influence of distant leaders is often mediated, their ability to manipulate is more feasible.

The book's discussion on "leadership signals" allows for clearer criteria of when a leader can be more trusted. This is directly related to the conflict which many thinkers in psychology believe is central in the human drama: the issue of dependence and independence.[27] Blind trust in large figures is, as discussed, a human default. This tendency can sometimes be dangerous, as it is particularly subject to emotional influences. Charismatic leaders have a particularly prominent ability in this area. Hitler, Jim Jones, and other prominent charismatic leaders excelled in their emotional expression. Being "in the spotlight", the center of attention, was a kind of life-saver for them – a response to narcissistic deprivation. The combination of a natural tendency to trust and experiencing exciting expressions of emotion can fuel dark forces.[28]

Seemingly, education for individuality and independence (certainly mental) is the answer to the dangers involved in blind trust in leaders.

However, as we have shown, group action and the ability to cooperate are what gave *Homo sapiens* a huge adaptive advantage. Therefore, it is difficult to ignore the evolutionary history, whose threads are hard-wired into the human "operating program". This program contains tendencies toward conformity and a large role for leadership, which reinforces the sense of groupness. There is also a conflict here. As Donald Winnicot[29] put it, the challenge is to advance in the "intermediate space" that expresses the individual's ability to be himself, separate, creative and independent, and yet dependent on and connected to others.

In order to understand the meaning of "intermediate space" and its relation to positive or negative charismatic leadership, one can think of a simple experience: a child playing hide-and-seek with one of his parents. The caring and wise parent hides where he knows the child can find him, in order to gratify and empower the child. This creates an experience of joy and pride in the child. In this situation, the child's sense of independence is encouraged and created through his dependence on the parent, and thanks to the parent's ability to be in the "right place" for him. That is, if the child is lucky, the authority figure – the large figure, on whom he depends (the parent) – does not "steal the show" (by choosing a difficult hiding place), but hands it over to the child ("You are wonderful! You found me!"). Thus, in this simple interaction, between an authority figure and one who is dependent on it, an "intermediary space" – between the necessary dependence and the important created independence – is developed. In this space, dependence and independence are not contradictory, but complementary, and can be achieved thanks to the authority figure's ability to give to the small figure. If we now recall the vertical evolutionary axis that leadership serves (e.g., natural pedagogy – passing on knowledge and practices), we can see this reflected in this simple interaction. The parent or leader fulfills his or her evolutionary role, passing on the baton to the next generation.

However, as we have seen, adaptive units of analysis are collective; therefore, we can also discuss trust in the broader social-systemic context through the following question: *Is it possible to produce trustworthy social systems that reduce the initial tendency to be blindly attracted to charismatic leaders?*

Indeed, differences in the level of systemic trust were found in comparative studies. For example, Japan was found to be a society characterized by the highest level of trust compared to any other society among the developed countries.[30] The high level of trust found among the Japanese is evident in people's trust in the "rules of the game", in the agreements signed between companies, trust in the managers of industrial and financial companies, and so on. Payments are paid on time, there is no need to sign a contract for everything (in all of Japan, which has 127 million inhabitants, there are fewer lawyers than in New York), things can be summed up over the phone, deliveries arrive on time, and so on. On the other hand, in societies characterized by a low level of trust (e.g., southern Italy), it is not even possible to raise donations to build a public library for the benefit of the town's residents for fear that the donations will find their way into the pockets of corrupt individuals. These differences have early historical origins. We pointed out some of them, such as the norms of cooperation among the rice growers or constitutive ties, such as the cooperation between the samurai who protected the rice growers in exchange for food supplies, and so on.

The interesting point for our discussion is the possibility that in a society characterized by a high degree of systemic trust, there will be less of a "leader-oriented tendency". This can be clearly seen from the literature published on successful organizations. In American literature, the success story is that of the "hero". Steve Jobs is the mythical and almost exclusive protagonist of "Apple"; Jack Welch is the savior and builder of General Electric; Lee Iacocca was the epitome of Chrysler's success. Endless stories of this type have appeared in magazines, on television, and on radio programs (some of which turned out to be a mythologization that did not match the facts).[31]

In Japan, on the other hand, for the most part, the story is "Sony's story", "Toyota's story" – the emphasis is always on the method, the norms, and the group; the leader is rarely the major story. In other words, there is room to wonder whether higher levels of systemic trust can reduce the tendency to need and admire charismatic leaders. Such collectives might be more resistant to the magic tricks of charisma, but might be more prone to excessive conformity. This is, of course, a speculative argument that largely concerns the question of whether individuals and certainly collectives can change, and if so, to what extent?

The changes that took place in both Germany and Japan after World War II engender hope for developmental processes along these lines. The third generation after the world war is obviously more distanced from the values of militaristic heroism than the generation which went through the war. Is this an example of Hegel's "cunning of reason" or is it simply a periodic phenomenon, which is hard to predict or define? The abundance of empirical evidence provides data that give encouraging weight to the developmental argument. Japan and Germany, as noted, are characterized by the highest level of systemic trust in the industrialized world.[32] The dramatic changes that took place in these societies after World War II raise the possibility that organizational and social arrangements have a place in the encouragement and empowerment of systemic trust.

Another contemplation that is more relevant to distant leaders, and perhaps especially to political leaders, is illustrated by the well-known example of Winston Churchill, who was (and is still considered to this day) the most charismatic leader – not only of Britain, but of the entire free world during World War II. As we noted earlier, although the most prominent charismatic figure of his time, Churchill was not elected prime minister in 1945 at the end of the war. His successor was a man less impressive in his rhetorical ability – a man considered unremarkable, modest, and quiet – the economist, Clement Attlee. When the British were asked: Why didn't you choose the charismatic and revered Churchill? They replied: "Churchill is a wartime leader. We now need a leader who will rehabilitate the economy."

This example is worth noting, as it actually presents the possibility that in a multi-generational perspective, followership can evolve and followers can also mature. That is, capabilities and criteria for identifying appropriate leadership can be developed. This example may not be coincidental. In other words, the ability to make inferences – both in relation to the circumstances and in relation to the processes and not just a reference to the personality of the leader – perhaps stems from the long-standing democratic traditions in Britain. In other words, as development of individuals, and the changes that take place during their lifetime, must be taken into account, it is perhaps possible and even important to better understand the development of collectives in this light.

EPILOGUE

As we have tried to show, there are endless discussions, studies, and interpretations regarding leadership and charisma. We have made an effort in this book to present an outline that organizes the complex discussion from the followers' perspective. We proposed an evolutionary-cultural perspective that clarifies the essence of the "charismatic fire", which forges individuals into coordinated and cohesive groups.

No single explanation here can suffice to answer the complex leadership "riddle". However, there is a point of view here that maintains that understanding the parts can help us to envisage the whole.

Thus, we can view the leadership phenomenon from various angles. From the biological, universal point of view, we can perceive humans and the leadership phenomenon as sharing some of the characteristics of the animal kingdom, and partly belonging to the social hierarchy typical of mammals, in general. We can see how our biology prepares us, in advance, to engage in cooperation and embrace social norms (as shown in natural pedagogy and epistemic trust studies). We have attempted to show that we carry within us innate tendencies of the human race (especially our sense of "groupness" and learning abilities), and that we continue to "grow" and develop our entire lives. In addition, although we are highly influenced by the biological perspective, we are often unaware of the fact that we are so sensitive to primary signals.

The leadership phenomenon may also be observed from the perspective of the sociologist and anthropologist, who perceive humans as symbolic creatures. These scientists observe human sensitivities to tribal affiliation, and notice how different signals affect different responses among different peoples. Moreover, they attempt to understand why people cry when they see a piece of cloth (the flag) of a certain color/pattern, and are indifferent to another piece of cloth of a different color/pattern; why some gather around a certain leader and others around another leader whose personality is radically different.

We can investigate the historian's perspective or that of the political scientist and ask "Why now?" What has become relevant at this point in time, and why does a symbol suddenly take on a particularly sweeping meaning? Why, at a certain moment in time, was a leader asked to return (de Gaulle, Dayan)? We can, of course, also don the spectacles of the psychologist, and attempt to analyze followers' information processing biases regarding leaders from the cognitive angle. We might also do well to use the psychological perspective to deal with issues such as motivation to lead.

The complexity of this issue is great, as was seen throughout this book. However, for those who strive for some sort of "bottom line" that might have practical implications, we will summarize as follows: The evolutionary observation points to defaults that are often biologically anchored. To demonstrate this in a somewhat simplistic, but common and current example – most people in the Western world (certainly those who are older in age) tend to gain weight. This is a type of default, whose biological origins are related to the need to conserve energy contained in sugars found in carbohydrates, due to the scarceness of food during early periods of human evolution. In other words, we are evolutionarily "wired" to consume foods that are high in sugar (as discussed in Chapter 2). However, understanding that this is a human default does not mean it is inevitable. As many overweight people know, this behavioral instinct can be overcome; but first, awareness is required, followed by a mobilization of willpower.

What is the moral of all this? Humans' tendency to "consume leaders" (of any kind, including spiritual guides, political leaders) is also a default whose primary source, as discussed, is ancient. However, this knowledge does not mean that this (dependence) tendency cannot be challenged, that is, that we cannot extend the range of our autonomy. This is, in fact, a derivative of the understanding that this is a biological-cultural evolutionary niche, within which there is constant interaction between biological determinism and our degree of choice. The key to the "game" between determinism and choice seems to be related to the awareness component.

The struggle against the default to be led requires understanding its causes. This aspect, in the leadership context, has not been thoroughly studied. Even experts, as we have indicated throughout the book, who study leadership as a psycho-social phenomenon, do so using concepts and tools of analysis that are not comprehensive enough to understand the nature, complexity, and especially the foundations of the followership–leadership phenomenon.

This claim is significant to understanding leadership *emergence*, as well as analyzing the *quality* of leadership. If there was more awareness of the biases we pointed out – and consequently, more intense socialization and learning processes in the field of leadership – then our ability, means, and criteria to examine leaders would have improved significantly. We would be far better equipped to answer the question: *Are the leaders we choose and follow truly deserving of our trust?*

Most of the effort that appears in the practical literature, in various training institutes and management schools, is focused on leaders and various methodologies of leadership development. However, if we return to the basic truth formulated by Bernard Bass[33] in such a clear and simple way: "There is no leader without followers", then, it is strongly recommended, as we have suggested, to remember also to reverse our perspective.

Our improvement as followers; our awareness of the ways and biases we apply when inferring about leaders; and our better judgement regarding our sources of trust in leaders can all significantly improve the leaders themselves. According to this claim, developing followers is largely the development of a better quality of leadership.

NOTES

1. Erikson, Erik, H. (1969). *On the Origins of Gandhi's Truth of Militant Non-Violence*. New York: W.W Norton & Co.
2. Pollack, Pam and Belviso, Meg (2014). *Who Was Nelson Mandela?* New York: Random House Penguin.
3. Gardner, John D. (2008). *In Search of Bill Clinton: A Psychological Biography*. New York: St Martin's Press.
4. Popper, Micha and Mayseless, Ofra (2003). Back to basics: Applying parenting perspective to transformational leadership. *Leadership Quarterly*, 14, 41–65.
5. Iremonger, Lucile (1970). *The Fiery Chariot*. London: Secker & Warburg.
6. Cox, Charles L. and Cooper, Cary, L. (1989). The making of the British CEO: Childhood, work experience, personality, and management style. *Academy of Management Executive*, 3, 241–5.
7. Elder, Glen H. (1974), *Children of the Great Depression*. Chicago, IL: University of Chicago Press.
8. Popper, Micha (2001). *Hypnotic Leadership*.
9. Popper, Micha (2005). *Leaders Who Transform Society: What Drives Them and Why We Are Attracted*. Westport, CT: Praeger.
10. Popper, Micha (2001). *Hypnotic Leadership*.
11. Bowlby, John (1969), *Attachment and Loss, Vol. 1: Attachment*. New York: Basic Books.
12. Fonagy, P. and Allison, Elizabeth (2014). The role of mentalizing and epistemic trust in the therapeutic relationship. *Psychotherapy*, 51(3), 372–80. doi:10.1037/a0036505.
13. An interview with Dr. Hai Inrojack (an expert on Tuurkey) in the *Haaretz* newspaper supplement, November 30, 2018 (Hebrew).
14. Diamond, Jared (1997). *Guns, Germs and Steel. The Fates of Human Societies*. New York: W.W. Norton & Co.
15. Maslow, Abraham (1970). *Motivation and Personality*. New York: Harper & Row.
16. Ingelhart, Ron F. (2018). *Cultural Evolution. People's Motivation Is Changing and Reshaping the World*. Cambridge: Cambridge University Press.
17. Hofstede, Geert (1997). *Cultures and Organizations. The Software of the Mind*. New York: McGraw-Hill.
18. Van Vugt, Mark, Hogan, Robert, and Kaiser, Robert B. (2008). Leadership, followership, and evolution. *American Psychologist*, 63(3), 182–96.
19. Shamir, Boas, House, Robert J., and Arthur, Michael B. (1993). The motivational effects of charismatic leadership: A self-concept based theory. *Organizational Science*, 4, 577–93.
20. Becker, Ernest (1973). *The Denial of Death*. New York: Free Press.

21. Boyd, Robert, Richerson, Peter J., and Henrich, Joseph (2011). The cultural niche: Why social learning is essential for human adaptation. *Proceedings of the National Academy of Sciences USA*, 108(Suppl. 2), 10918–25.
22. Lampert, Ada (1997). *The Evolution of Love*. Westport, CT: Praeger.
23. Popper, Micha and Castelnovo, Omri (2019). The primary foundations of followership. *Journal for the Theory of Social Behaviour*. doi: 10.1111/jtsb.12209.
24. Argyris, C. (1993). *Knowledge for Action: A Guide to Overcoming Barriers to Organizational Change*. San Francisco, CA: Jossey-Bass.
25. Gladwell, Malcolm (2019). *Talking to Strangers*. London: Penguin Books.
26. Ibid., p. 157.
27. Winnicot, Donald (1965). *The Maturational Processes and the Facilitating Environment*. London: Routledge.
28. Popper, *Hypnotic Leadership*.
29. Winnicot, *The Maturational Processes*.
30. Fukuyama, Francis (1995). *Trust. The Social Virtues and the Creation of Prosperity*. New York: Free Press.
31. Spector, Bert (2013). Flawed from the "get-go": Lee Iacocca and the origins of transformational leadership. *Leadership*, 10(3), 361–79.
32. Fukuyama, Francis (1995). *Trust*. New York: Free Press.
33. Bass, Bernard. M. (1985). *Leadership and Performance beyond Expectations*. New York: Free Press.

References

Allison, Scott T. and Goethals, George R. (2011). *Heroes: What They Do and Why We Need Them*. New York: Oxford University Press.

Antonakis, John and Dalgas, Olaf (2009). Predicting elections: Child's play. *Science*, 232 (February), 1183.

Antonakis, J., Bastardoz, N., Jacquart, P., and Shamir, B. (2016). Charisma: An ill-defined and ill-measured gift. *Annual Review of Organizational Psychology and Organizational Behavior*, 3, 293–319.

Argyris, Chris (1993). *Knowledge for Action: A Guide to Overcoming Barriers to Organizational Change*. San Francisco, CA: Jossey-Bass.

Asch, Solomon (1946). Framing impressions of personality. *Journal of Abnormal and Social Psychology*, 41, 258–90.

Avolio, Bruce, Bass, Bernard M., and Jung, Dong I. (1999). Re-examining the components of transformational and transactional leadership using the Multifactor Leadership Questionnaire. *Journal of Occupational and Organizational Psychology*, 72, 441–62.

Bailly, Jean-Sylvian (2002). Secret Report on Mesmerism or Animal Magnetism. *International Journal of Clinical and Experimental Hypnosis*, 50(4) (October), 364–8.

Bandura, Albert (1982). Human agency in social cognitive theory. *American Psychologist*, 44, 1175–84.

Banfield, Edward (1958). *The Moral Basis of Backward Society*. Glancoe, IL: Free Press.

Bass, Bernard M. (1985). *Leadership and Performance beyond Expectations*. New York: Free Press.

Bass, Bernard M. (2008). *The Bass Handbook of Leadership*, 4th edn. New York: Free Press.

Becker, Ernest (1973). *The Denial of Death*. New York: Free Press.

Best, Geoffrey (2003). *Churchill: A Study in Greatness*. New York: Oxford University Press.

Boehm, Christopher (1999). *Hierarchy in the Forest*. London: Harvard University Press.

Botticini, Maristella and Eckstein, Zvi (2012). *The Chosen Few: How Education Shaped Jewish History*. Princeton, NJ: Princeton University Press.

Bowlby, John (1969). *Attachment and Loss, Vol. 1: Attachment*. New York: Basic Books.

Bowlby, John (1973). *Attachment and Loss, Vol. 2: Separation*. New York: Basic Books.

Bowlby, John (1980). *Attachment and loss, Vol. 3: Loss, Sadness and Depression*. New York: Basic Books.

Boyd, Robert and Richerson, Peter (1988). *Culture and Evolutionary Process.* Chicago, IL: University of Chicago Press.

Boyd, Robert and Richerson, Peter J. (2005). *The Origin and Evolution of Cultures.* Oxford: Oxford University Press.

Boyd, Robert, Richerson, Peter J. and Henrich, Joseph (2011). The cultural niche: Why social learning is essential for human adaptation. *Proceedings of the National Academy of Sciences USA,* 108(Suppl. 2), 10918–25.

Brosh, Tamar (1993). *Neum lechol et (Speech at all times).* Tel Aviv: Yediot Sefarim (Hebrew).

Bruner, Jerome (1986). *Actual Minds, Possible Worlds.* Cambridge, MA: Harvard University Press.

Burns, James MacGregor (1978). *Leadership.* New York: Harper & Row.

Buss, David (1989). Sex differences in human mate preferences: Evolutionary hypotheses tested in 37 cultures. *Behavioral and Brain Sciences,* 12, 1–49.

Buttelmann, David, Zmyj, Norbert, Daum, Moritz, and Carpenter, Malinda (2013). Selective imitation of in-group over out-group members in 14-month-old infants. *Child Development,* 84(2), 422–8.

Campbell, John K. (1970). Honor and the devil. In J.G. Peristiany (ed.), *Honor and Shame: The Values of Mediterranean Society.* Chicago, IL University of Chicago Press, pp. 141–70.

Carlyle, Thomas (1841). *On Heroes, Hero-Worship and the Heroic in History,* reprinted 1907. Boston: Houghton Mifflin.

Cassidy, Jude and Shaver, Philip (eds) (2018). Handbook *of Attachment. Theory, Research and Clinical Applications.* 3rd edn. New York: Guilford Publications.

Castelnovo, Omri, Popper, Micha, and Koren, Danny (2017). The innate code of charisma. *Leadership Quarterly,* 28, 543–54.

Conger, Jay A. and Kanungo, Rabindra N. (1987). Toward a behavioral theory of charismatic leadership in organizational settings. *Academy of Management Review,* 12, 637–47.

Connor, Walker (1994). *Ethno-Nationalism: The Quest of Understanding.* Princeton, NJ: Princeton University Press.

Cox, Charles J. and Cooper, Cary L. (1989). The making of the British CEO: Childhood, work experience, personality, and management style. *Academy of Management Executive,* 3, 241–5.

Csibra, Gergely and Gergely, Gyorgy (2006). Social learning and social cognition: The case for pedagogy. Processes of change in brain and cognitive development. *Attention and Performance,* 21, 249–74.

Csibra, Gergely and Gergely, Gyorgy (2009). Natural pedagogy. *Trends in Cognitive Sciences,* 13, 148–53.

Csibra, Gergely and Gergely, Gyorgy (2011). Natural pedagogy as evolutionary adaptation. *Philosophical Transactions of the Royal Society of London B: Biological Sciences,* 366(1567), 1149–57.

Dawkins, Richard (1999) Introduction to Susan Blackmore's book: *The Meme Machine.* Oxford: Oxford University Press.

De Dreu, Caresten K. and Kret, Mariska E. (2015). Oxytocin conditions inter-group relations through unregulated in-group empathy, cooperation, conformity and defense. *Biological Psychiatry*, 79(3), 165–73.

Derks, Bella, Sheepers, Daan, and Ellemers, Naomi (eds) (2013). *Neuroscience of Prejudice and Intergroup Relations*. New York: Psychology Press.

Diamond, Jared (1997). *Guns, Germs and Steel. The Fates of Human Societies*. New York: W.W. Norton & Co.

Disendruck, Gil and Weiss, Eitan (2015). Differential weighting of cues to social categories. *Cognitive Development*, 33, 56–72.

Drath, Wilfred H., McCauley, Cintya D., Palus, Charles J. et al. (2008). Direction, alignment, commitment: Toward a more integrative ontology of leadership. *Leadership Quarterly*, 19, 635–53.

Durkheim, Emile (1973). The dualism of human nature and its social conditions. In R. Bellah (ed.), *Emile Durkheim on Morality and Society*. Chicago, IL: University of Chicago Press.

Elon, Amos (2004). *Pity It All: A Portrait of Jews in Germany, 1743–1933*. New York: Penguin Books.

Emerson, Alfred (1946). The biological basis of social cooperation. *Illinois Academy of Science Transactions*, 39, 12.

Erikson, Erik H. (1969). *On the Origins of Gandhi's Truth of Militant Non-Violence*. New York: W.W. Norton & Co.

Feldman, Ruth (2007). Parent–infant synchrony and the construction of shared timing; physiological precursors, developmental outcomes, and risk conditions. *Journal of Child Psychology and Psychiatry*, 48(3–4), 329–54.

Feldman, R., Magori-Cohen, R., Galili, G., Singer, M., and Louzoun, Y. (2011). Mother and infant coordinate heart rhythms through episodes of interaction synchrony. *Infant Behavior and Development*, 34(4), 569–77.

Fisher, Ronald A. (1930). *The General Theory of Natural Selection*. Cambridge: Cambridge University Press.

Fiske, Susan T., Cuddy, Amy J.C., and Glick, Peter (2007). Universal dimensions of social cognition: Warmth and competence. *Trends in Cognitive Sciences*, 11(2), 77–83.

Fonagy, Peter and Elizabeth Allison (2014). The role of mentalizing and epistemic trust in the therapeutic relationship. *Psychotherapy*, 51(3), 372–80.

Fukuyama, Francis (1995). *Trust. The Social Virtues and the Creation of Prosperity*. New York: Free Press.

Gabriel, Richard A. and Savage, Paul L. (1978). *Crisis in Command*. New York: Hill and Wang.

Gardiner, Amy K., Greif, Marissa L., and Bjorklund, David F. (2011). Guided by intention: Preschoolers' imitation reflects inferences of causation. *Journal of Cognition and Development*, 12(3), 355–73.

Gardner, John D. (2008). *In Search of Bill Clinton: A Psychological Biography*. New York: St Martin's Press.

Gardner, William, Cogliser, C.C., Davis, Kelly M., and Dickens, Matthew P. (2011). Authentic leadership: A review of the literature and research agenda. *Leadership Quarterly*, 22, 1120–45.

Gat, Azar (2013). *Nations: The Long History of Deep Roots of Political Ethnicity and Nationalism*. New York: Cambridge University Press.

Gellner, Ernest (2006). *Nations and Nationalism*, 2nd edn. Ithaca, NY: Cornell University Press.

Gergely, Gyorgey and Jacob, Pierr (2012). Reasoning about instrumental and communicative agency in human infancy. *Advances in Child Development and Behavior*, 43, 59–94.

Gerstner, Charlotte and Day, David (1994). Cross cultural comparisons of leadership prototypes. *Leadership Quarterly*, 5, 121–34.

Gladwell, Malcolm (2005). *Blink. The Power of Thinking without Thinking*. London: Penguin Books.

Gladwell, Malcolm (2008). *Outliers*. New York: Little Brown and Company, p. 154.

Gladwell, Malcolm (2019). *Talking to Strangers*. London: Penguin Books.

Glen, H. (1974). *Children of the Great Depression*. Chicago, IL: University of Chicago Press.

Goldhagen, Daniel Jonah (1996). *Ordinary Germans and the Holocaust*. New York: Alfred A. Knopf.

Grossmann, Tobias (2013). The role of medial prefrontal cortex in early social cognition. *Frontiers in Human Neuroscience*, 7, 340.

Gutmann, Amy (ed.) (1994). *Multiculturalism: Examining the Politics of Recognition*. Princeton, NJ: Princeton University Press.

Haaretz newspaper supplement (2018). Interview with Dr. Hai Eitan Inrojack, November 30, p. 24.

Halbwachs, Maurice (1926). *The Collective Memory*, reprinted 1950, trans. F.J. and V.Y. Ditter. London: Harper Colophon Books.

Haldane, John Burdon (1935). *The Philosophy of a Biologist*. Oxford: Clarendon Press.

Halperin, Eran (2014). Emotion, emotion regulation, and conflict resolution. *Emotion Review*, 6(1), 68–76.

Harari, Yuval N. (2015). *Sapiens: A Brief History of Humankind*. New York: Harper and Collins.

Harman, Oren (2011). *The Price of Altruism and the Search for the Origins of Kindness*. W.W. Norton & Co.

Hasson, Uri, Ghazanfar, Asif A., Galantucci, Bruno, Garrod, Simon, and Keysers, Christian (2012). Brain-to-brain coupling: A mechanism for creating and sharing a social world. *Trends in Cognitive Sciences*, 16(2), 114–21.

Hazan, Cindy and Shaver, Philip (1987). Romantic love conceptualized as an attachment process. *Journal of Personality and Social Psychology*, 52, 511–24.

Henrich, Joseph (2009). The evolution of costly displays, cooperation and religion: Credibility enhancing displays and their implications for cultural evolution. *Evolution and Human Behavior*, 30(4), 244–60.

Henrich, Joseph, Heine, Steven, and Norenzayan, Ara (2010). The weirdest people in the world? *Behavioral and Brain Sciences*, 33, 61–135.

Hertzler, J.O. (1940). Crises and dictatorships. *American Sociological Review*, 5, 157–69.

Hill, Melvinu A. (1984). The law of the father: Leadership and symbolic authority in psychoanalysis. In B. Kellerman (ed.), *Leadership: Multidisciplinary Perspectives*. Englewood Cliffs, NJ: Prentice Hall, pp. 128–40.

Hitler, Adolf (2018) *Mein Kampf* (Vol. 1), trans. Thomas Dalton. New York, Clemens and Blair, p. 352.

Hofstede, Geert (1997). *Cultures and Organizations: The Software of the Mind*. New York: McGraw-Hill, p. 7.

Howard, Jonathan (1982). *Darwin*. Oxford: Oxford University Press.

Ingelhart, Ron F. (2018). *Cultural Evolution. People's Motivation Is Changing and Reshaping the World*. Cambridge: Cambridge University Press.

Iremonger, Lucile (1970). *The Fiery Chariot*. London: Secker & Warburg.

Kafashan, Sara, Sparks, Adam, Rotella, Amanda, and Barclay, Pat (2017). Why heroism exists. Evoutionary perspectives on external helping. In Allison Scott, George Goethals, and Roderick M. Kramer (eds), *Handbook of Heroism and Heroic Leadership*. New York: Routledge, pp. 36–58.

Kahneman, Daniel (2017). *Thinking Fast and Slow*. New York: Farrar, Straus & Giroux.

Kahneman, Daniel, and Tversky, Amos (1972). Subjective probability: A judgment of representativeness. *Cognitive Psychology*, 3, 430–54.

Kenrick, Douglas T. and Griskevicius, Vladas (2013). *The Rational Animal. How Evolution Made Us Smarter Than We think*. New York: Basic Books.

Kenrick, Douglas T. and Keefe, Richard C. (1992). Age preferences in mates reflect sex differences in human reproductive strategies. *Behavioral and Brain Sciences*, 15, 75–133.

Kenrick, Douglas T., Keefe, Richard C., Bryan, Angella, Barr, Alicia, and Brown, Stephanie (1995). Age preferences and mate choice among heterosexuals: A case for modular psychological mechanisms. *Journal of Personality and Social Psychology*, 69, 1166–72.

Kershaw, Ian (1998). *Hitler, 1889–1936: Hubris*. London: Penguin Books.

Kets de Vries, Manfred (1988). Prisoners of leadership. *Human Relations*, 41(31), 261–80.

Kim, Heejung and Markus, Hazel R. (1999). Deviance or uniqueness, harmony or conformity? A cultural analysis. *Journal of Personality and Social Psychology*, 77(4), 785–800.

Kinreich, Sivan, Djalovski, Amir, Kraus, Lior, Louzoun, Yoram, and Feldman, Ruth (2017). Brain-to-brain synchrony during naturalistic social interactions. *Scientific Reports*, 7(1), 1–12.

Klein, Katherine and House, Robert (1995). On fire: Charismatic leadership and level of analysis. *Leadership Quarterly*, 6(2), 183–98.

Kosinski, Jersey (1972). *Being There*. New York: Bantam Books.

Lakshminarayanan, Venkat M., Chen, Keith, and Santos, Laurie (2008). Endowment effect in Capuchin monkeys. *Philosophical Transactions of the Royal Society B: Biological Sciences*, 363, 3837–44.

Lampert. Ada (1997). *The Evolution of Love*. Westport, CT: Praeger.

Laurence, Janice H. and Mathews, Michael D. (2012). *The Oxford Handbook of Military Psychology*. New York: Oxford University Press.

Lewin, Kurt (1947). Frontiers in group dynamics: Concept, method, and reality in social science. *Human Relations*, 1, 5–42.

Lewis, Michael (2016). *The Undoing Project. A Friendship That Changed Our Mind*. New York: Norton.

Liberman, Nira, Trope, Yaakov, and Stephan, Elena (2007). Psychological distance. In A.W. Kruglanski and E.T. Higgins (eds), *Social Psychology: Handbook of Basic Principles*. New York: Guilford Press, pp. 353–81.

Liker, Jeffrey and Hoseus, Michael (2008). *Toyota Culture: The Heart and Soul of the Toyota Way*. New York: McGraw-Hill.

Lindholm, Charles (1988). Lovers and leaders. *Social Science Information*, 27(1) (March), 3–45.

LoBue, Vanessa, DeLoach, Judy S. (2008). Detecting snake in the grass: Attention to fear-relevant stimuli by adults and young children. *Psychological Science*, 19(3), 284–9.

Markus, Hazel and Wurf, Elissa (1987). The dynamic self-concept: A social-psychological perspective. *Annual Review of Psychology*, 38, 299–337.

Maslow, Abraham (1970). *Motivation and Personality*. New York: Harper & Row.

Mayseless, Ofra and Popper, Micha (2019). Attachment and leadership: Review and new insights. *Current Opinion in Psychology*, February 25, 157–71.

Mayseless, Ofra, Sharabany, Ruth, and Sagi, Avi (1997). Attachment concerns of others as manifested in parental, spousal and friendship relationships. *Personal Relationships*, 4, 255–69.

McDonough, Frank (2019). *The Hitler Years: Triumph 1933–1939*. London. Head of Zeus, p. 64.

Meindl, James R. (1995). The romance of leadership as follower-centric theory: A social constructivist approach. *Leadership Quarterly*, 6, 329–41.

Meindl, James R., Ehrlich, Sanford B., and Dukerich, Janet M. (1985). The romance of leadership. *Administrative Science Quarterly*, 30, 78–102.

Meltzoff, Andrew N. (1988). Infant imitation after a 1-week delay: Long-term memory for novel acts and multiple stimuli. *Developmental Psychology*, 24(4), 470.

Mintzberg, Henry (1973). *The Nature of Managerial Work*. New York: Harper & Row.

Mintzberg, Henry (1979). *The Structuring of Organizations: A Synthesis of the Research*. Englewood Cliffs, NJ: Prentice Hall.

Mizrahi, Yoni (2009). Introduction to Suzan Blackmore's book: *The Meme Machine*. Kineret, Zmora – Bitan, Dvir Publishing House and Yezreel Academic Press (Hebrew).

Nisbett, Richard E. and Cohen, Dov (1996). *Culture of Honor: The Psychology of Violence in the South*. Boulder, CO: Westview Press.

Olivola, Christopher Y. and Todorov, Alexander (2010). Elected in 100 milliseconds: Appearance-based trait. Inference and voting. *Journal of Nonverbal Behavior*, 34, 83–110.

Panksepp, Jaak (1998). *Affective Neuroscience: The Foundations of Human and Animal Emotions*. Oxford: Oxford University Press.

Pollack, Pam and Belviso, Meg (2014). *Who Was Nelson Mandela?* New York: Random House Penguin.

Popper, Micha (2001). *Hypnotic Leadership*. Westport, CT: Praeger.

Popper, Micha (2005). *Leaders Who Transform Society: What Drives Them and Why We Are Attracted*. Westport, CT: Praeger.

Popper, Micha (2012). *Fact and Fantasy about Leadership*. Cheltenham, UK and Northampton, MA, USA: Edward Elgar.

Popper, Micha (2013). Leaders perceived as distant or close: Some implications for psychological theory on leadership. *Leadership Quarterly*, 24, 1–8.

Popper, Micha (2016). Followership, deity and leadership. *Journal for the Theory of Social Behaviour*, 46(2), 211–28.

Popper, Micha and Castelnovo, Omri. (2018). The function of great leaders in human culture: A cultural-evolutionary perspective. *Leadership*, 14(6), 757–74.

Popper, Micha and Castelnovo, Omri (2019). The primary foundations of followership. *Journal for the Theory of Social Behaviour*. doi: 10.1111/jtsb.12209.

Popper, Micha and Mayseless, Ofra (2003). Back to basics: Applying parenting perspective to transformational leadership. *Leadership Quarterly*, 14, 41–65.

Reed, John Shelton (1982). *One South: An Ethnic Approach to Regional Culture*. Baton Rouge, LA: Louisiana State University Press.

Schjoedt, Uffe, Stødkilde-Jørgensen, Hans, Geertz, Armin. W., Lund, Torben E., and Roepstorff, Andreas (2010). The power of charisma: Perceived charisma inhibits the frontal executive network of believers in intercessory prayer. *Social Cognitive and Affective Neuroscience*, nsq023.

Schlesinger, Arthur M. Jr. (1958). *The Coming of the New Deal*. Boston: Houghton Mifflin, pp. 1–2.

Schwartz, Barry (2000). *Abraham Lincoln. Forge of National Memory*. Chicago, IL: University of Chicago Press.

Segal, Marshal H., Campbell, Donald T., and Herskovits, Melville J. (1966). *The Influence of Culture on Visual Perception*. Indiana, IN: Bobbs-Merrill.

Shalit, Alon, Popper, Micha, and Zakay, Dan (2010). Followers' attachment styles and their preference for social or personal charismatic leaders. *Leadership and Organizational Development Journal*, 31(5), 458–72.

Shamir, Boas (1995). Social distance and charisma. Theoretical notes and explanatory study. *Leadership Quarterly*, 1, 19–48.

Shamir, Boas (2007). From passive recipients to active co-producers: Followers' role in the leadership process. In B. Shamir, R. Pillai, M.C. Bligh, and M. Uhl-Bien (eds), *Follower-Centered Perspectives on Leadership*. Greenwich, CT: Information Publishing, pp. ix–xxxix.

Shamir, Boas, House, Robert J., and Arthur, Michael B. (1993). The motivational effects of charismatic leadership: A self-concept based theory. *Organizational Science*, 4, 577–93.

Shamir, Boas, Arthur, Michael B., and House, Robert J. (1994). The rhetoric of charismatic leadership: A theoretical extension, a case study and implications for research. *Leadership Quarterly*, 5(1), 25.

Shapira, Anita (1997). *Yheudim Hadashim Yehudim Yeshanim (New Jews Old Jews)*. Tel Aviv: Sifriat Ofakim. Am Oved (Hebrew).

Shechter, Rivka (1990). *The Theological Foundations of the Third Reich*. Tel Aviv: Ministry of Defense Publishing (Hebrew).

Shteynberg, Garriy (2010). A silent emergence of culture: The social tuning effect. *Journal of Personality and Social Psychology*, 99(4), 683.

Skinner, Fredrick (1965). *Science and Human Behavior*. New York: Free Press.

Smith, Anthony D. (1986). *The Ethnic Origins of Nations*. Oxford: Blackwell.

Spector, Bert (2013). Flawed from the "get-go": Lee Iacocca and the origins of transformational leadership. *Leadership*, 10(3), 361–79.

Storr, Anthony (1972). *The Dynamics of Creation*. London: Secker & Warburg.

Tallhelm, Thomas, Zhang, Xuemin, Oishi, Shige et al. (2014). Large-scale psychological differences within China explained by rice versus wheat agriculture. *Science*, 344(6184), 603–8.

Tawney, Richard H. (1962). *Religion and the Rise of Capitalism*. New York: Harcourt Brace.

Todorov, Alexander, Mandisodza, Ansu, Goren, Amir, and Hall, Crysta C. (2005). Inferences of competence from faces predict election outcomes. *Science*, 308 (June), 1623–6.

Tomasello, Michael (2014). *A Natural History of Human Thinking*. Cambridge, MA: Harvard University Press.

Tomasello, Michael and Rakoczy, Hanes (2003). What makes human cognition unique? From individual to shared to collective intentionality. *Mind and Language*, 18, 121–47.

Tversky, Amos and Kahneman, Daniel (1981). The framing of decisions and the psychology of choice. *Science*, 211, 453–8.

Vamik,Volkan (2016). *Siblings*. Charlottesville, VA: Pitchstone Publishing.

Van Vugt, M. and Grabo, Allen E. (2015). The many faces of leadership: An evolutionary-psychology approach. *Current Directions in Psychological Science*, 24(6), 484–9.

Van Vugt, Mark, Hogan, Robert, and Kaiser, Robert B. (2008). Leadership, followership, and evolution. *American Psychologist*, 63(3), 182–96.

Waal, Frans B.M. de (1996). *Good Natured*. Cambridge, MA: Harvard University Press.

Weber, Max (1924). *The Theory of Social and Economic Organization*, reprinted 1947, trans. Talcott Parsons. New York: Free Press.

Weber, Max (1968). *Economy and Society*. New York: Bedminster Press.

Wilson, Deirdre and Sperber, Dan (2012). *Meaning and Relevance*. Cambridge: Cambridge University Press.

Winnicot, Donald (1965). *The Maturational Processes and the Facilitating Environment*. London: Routledge.

Woodward, Bob (2018). *Fear: Trump in the White House*. New York: Simon & Schuster.

Zahavi, Amotz and Zahavi, Avishag (1997). *The Handicap Principle: A Missing Piece of Darwin's Puzzle*. New York: Oxford University Press.

Zajonc, Robert B. (1980). Feelings and thinking, preferences need no inferences. *American Psychologist*, 35(2), 151–175.

Index

Leadership and charisma